I0815573

52 PRAYERS FOR MY WIFE

TYNDALE
MOMENTUM®

A Tyndale nonfiction imprint

52 PRAYERS FOR MY WIFE

A DEVOTIONAL

CALEB ROUSE

Visit Tyndale online at tyndale.com.

Visit Tyndale Momentum online at tyndalemomentum.com.

Tyndale, Tyndale's quill logo, *Tyndale Momentum*, and the Tyndale Momentum logo are registered trademarks of Tyndale House Ministries. Tyndale Momentum is a nonfiction imprint of Tyndale House Publishers, Carol Stream, Illinois.

52 Prayers for My Wife: A Devotional

Published in association with The Bindery Agency, www.TheBinderyAgency.com.

Designed by Sarah Susan Richardson

Edited by Donna L. Berg

For information about special discounts for bulk purchases, please contact Tyndale House Publishers at csresponse@tyndale.com, or call 1-855-277-9400.

ISBN 979-8-4005-0108-1

Printed in China

30 29 28 27 26 25 24
7 6 5 4 3 2 1

To my amazing wife, Stefanie,

you inspire me every day to be a better man, husband, and follower of Jesus. Thank you for encouraging me to love God more and for sparking this dream of mine to help people across the world in their marriages and relationships. This book is possible because of your initial dream and your willingness to pursue the call God has placed on your life. You are forever my princess, the woman of my dreams, and I fall more deeply in love with you every single day. This book is for you.

And to you, the husband holding this book and reading these words, you got this!

Marriage is an incredible gift, and I am so proud of you for taking this step to intercede for your wife before the Father. Your future changes every time you pray for her. Don't give up, go to God first, and watch Him work all things together for your good. I pray this book encourages you, uplifts you, and challenges you to be the best husband you can possibly be. God is with you through it all.

Introduction

Dear beloved reader,

My wife, Stefanie, and I have made a point of keeping prayer as the foundation of our relationship. Some days, neither of us has anything left to give the other person, but God provides the strength we need. We've experienced the power of prayer and the amazing way God can transform our lives and relationship when we bring our concerns to Him. He's been with us all along, through both the good and the difficult days.

As a husband, I have sometimes been tempted to try and fix my wife. I lacked humility and wasn't a good listener. I still catch myself struggling with this at times. This only gets in the way of what God wants to do in us. The more I learn about surrendering my wife to God and looking for the best in her, the more I thrive in my marriage and in life. I believe that your marriage, too, can become even more fulfilling over time as you pour your energies into prayer for your wife.

I look forward to embarking on this journey of spiritual and marital growth with you. As a Christian relationship coach with a passion for nurturing marriages, I've created this guide to help you strengthen the bond between yourself and your wife through the power of prayer and purposeful action. My hope is that we as husbands can grow to be more like Jesus through this journey—to be men who increasingly honor, respect, and love our wives.

Marriage is a beautiful gift from God, but it requires intentional effort and continuous nourishment to thrive. Prayer is a dynamic force that can transform both *your* heart and your wife's heart, leading to a more fulfilling and God-centered marriage. Prayer is not just a passive request but a powerful tool for transformation. As you pray, you invite God to work within you and your marriage, aligning your desires with His will. With purposeful prayer, you can watch your relationship grow stronger and healthier, knowing that you are partnering with the Creator of love and marriage.[1]

This devotional is designed to be a weekly companion for your journey. Each week, you'll find a specific topic for prayer and reflection, including your wife's spiritual growth, her physical and emotional well-being, her relationship with you, and her relationships with others.

At the top of the page, you'll find Scripture that goes along with the topic. Memorizing or meditating on these verses each week is a helpful way to remind yourself of God's truth that trumps our emotions and circumstances.

Next, I'll share a personal story of how prayer has played a role in my own marriage as we've dealt with the particular topic. I'm sure that many of the issues we've struggled with will sound familiar to you. I hope it will encourage you to know that these are common to many relationships. After my story, you'll find a suggested prayer for the topic, helping you to pray specifically, intentionally, and with purpose for the daily needs of your wife.

You will also find a summarizing word of encouragement intended to help you keep the topic at the front of your mind throughout the week. You might want to write it on a sticky note so you remember to put the topic into practice every day.

In addition to prayer, I've included practical "Love in Action"

---

1 You might also be interested in our companion book, *52 Prayers for My Husband: A Devotional*, written by my wife, Stefanie, in case you and your wife would like to join efforts on this journey.

suggestions for each week, which are designed to help you apply the principles discussed in each devotional. These calls to action begin with one special activity you can do together with your wife. However, I understand that every marriage is unique, and in case your wife seems resistant or uninterested, I've also included a second activity that you can do on her behalf, which does not require her participation. The goal is to invest in your marriage and demonstrate love in tangible ways. In any case, be sure your wife knows you are praying for her regularly, which will be a big encouragement to her.

It is my hope that this approach allows you to immerse yourself fully in the topic, giving you time to pray earnestly for your wife to flourish in various aspects of life, as well as for you to grow as a husband as you seek to support her.

I encourage you to embrace this prayer guide with an open heart, knowing that growth takes time and patience. As you pray for your wife, don't be surprised if you see changes in your own life as well. Each devotional is an opportunity to deepen your connection with God and with each other. It's an invitation to seek God's wisdom, guidance, and blessings for your marriage.

I want to walk alongside you on this journey. I believe in the power of prayer and the potential for transformation. It is my sincere hope that this guide will inspire you, uplift your spirit, and breathe new life into your relationship.

May your journey through this guide be filled with love, grace, and the presence of God. May your marriage be a testament to His goodness and faithfulness. Together, let's nurture the love that God has planted in your heart and watch it flourish as you commit to a year of prayerful growth.

With love and blessings,

Caleb Rouse
Christian relationship coach

WEEK 1

LEARNING TO LISTEN

A prayer that her need for emotional support is met

Understand this, my dear brothers and sisters: You must all be quick to listen, slow to speak, and slow to get angry.

JAMES 1:19

Early in our marriage, I tried to fix everything for Stefanie. When she brought up a concern to me, my mind would immediately go to all the ways that I needed to handle the problem for her.

We used to work as teachers at the same Christian school in California. On occasion, when she shared with me about difficulties that would arise at the school, I would immediately try to correct the problem. Other times, I would express to her that the way she was experiencing the difficulty was wrong and that the people involved probably didn't intend their actions to be taken the way she was interpreting them.

While this may or may not have been the best response, the problem was that she didn't feel heard. Instead, she felt that I was just trying to fix her or was taking the other side. This led to conflict and frustration between us. What I learned over time (and with practice) was that she wanted me to listen, to affirm that her feelings were valid, and to show her support in what she was doing well.

Developing this skill was not easy, but it has brought peace and understanding to our marriage. It was also freeing for me not to feel like I had to fix everything. This unlocked the door to her heart and built trust between us over time.

Dear God, I thank You for this amazing woman I get to do life with. *She is a blessing to me. I pray that she would find her needs met, first and foremost, through her relationship with You. I pray also that You would give me wisdom to know her needs and to do what I can to take care of them. As she shares her frustrations with me, help me to listen with patience and respond in gentleness. Teach me to listen before I speak and to pay attention to the desires of her heart.*

I pray that in our daily interactions, I would be attuned to what she is saying verbally and nonverbally. Show me ways that I can pray for her and communicate clearly with her. When I have frustrations, show me how to express how I feel rather than just bottling up my emotions. I ask that You would provide her with the grace to be patient with me. Help us to fall more in love with You and with each other every day. In the name of Jesus, amen.

Your wife wants to know you care about her feelings in a situation more than you care about her getting over it.

love in action . . .

Together: Talk about situations that have been difficult to deal with. Give each other space for fully expressing feelings, and show unwavering support.

—— • ——

For her: When your wife brings up something that is frustrating her, choose to listen, validate her feelings, and show your support.

WEEK

2

THE POWER OF A TIMELY WORD

A prayer that she finds the encouragement she needs

Encourage one another and build each other up, just as in fact you are doing.

1 THESSALONIANS 5:11, NIV

My lifelong dream was to be a professional basketball player. I was "all in" from middle school through college. I lived, breathed, and walked basketball, often forgoing everything else. But in my senior year of college, I had a career-ending injury one day in practice that would forever alter my life.

Depressed, discouraged, and dismayed, I stumbled through the next ten years with little purpose. When I met Stefanie, I learned a new story. Her walk with the Lord encouraged me to take action toward gratefulness and daily time with Him.

Through her encouragement (it took a lot), I learned to find my worth in God, rather than in my broken dreams. I began to choose thankfulness each day over disappointment. It led me to find a new dream and passion in helping others to build strong marriages. Through my mistakes, pains, and hurts, Stefanie consistently loved and supported me. I only pray that I can be as much of an encouragement to her as she has been for me.

There is power in the encouragement of others. Consider whether there are areas in which your wife could use encouragement today. Perhaps she is facing frustrations or broken dreams. Look for ways to love her through your words.

Heavenly Father, I pray that You would encourage my wife in spite of any frustrating situations or broken dreams she may be battling. *Help her to be aware of the many blessings You have given us and to have a sense of gratitude for them. In every situation, may I encourage her and point her toward You. Father, let me be a person who gives her perspective in difficult times. I pray that when she gets discouraged, she will remember that I am here to support her.*

Help me to never take my wife for granted. I pray that as I love her, she would feel special. I pray that I can be a blessing to her today in the way that she needs it the most. Encourage me to be consistent with my kindness and gentleness toward her. Let thankfulness far outweigh bitterness in our household. Teach us to run to You in all circumstances, and help me to be a grateful and peaceful husband to my wife. Amen.

A word of encouragement at the right moment can renew hope.

love in action . . .

Together: Take turns sharing at least three encouraging comments about what you appreciate about each other.

—— • ——

For her: Make a point of letting your wife know how much you appreciate her and why.

WEEK

3

REMINDING HER OF HER VALUE

A prayer that she will know her worth in Christ

Seek the Kingdom of God above all else, and live righteously, and he will give you everything you need.

MATTHEW 6:33

We have faced difficulties in our marriage countless times. Whether it's with family dynamics, friendship hurts, work difficulties, lies spoken about us, or even major disappointments, we have experienced hurt.

Little else causes me as much pain as seeing Stefanie's heart broken. Something instinctive kicks in, and I want to run to her rescue. Those hurtful moments can cause anyone to doubt themselves, question their worth, and sometimes run away emotionally or physically from those around them. When those moments happen to our wives, we have the opportunity to bring life, hope, and worth to them.

With Stefanie, I find that when I pull her close to me, let her know I love her, speak God's truth from Scripture over her, and listen to her, she is able to see clearly through whatever she is facing and claim the truth.

Dear God, I lift up my wife's heart today. *Protect her heart from evil and guide her to Your truth each day. When lies come up and cause her to doubt You or to lose confidence, I pray she runs to Your Word. Help me to always point her back to Your truth to sustain her, guide her, and give her peace.*

So many things in this world can push her away from You and cause her to seek her worth in other things. I pray that when this happens, You would remind her that she is Your child, that she has value, and that her worth comes from You alone. I know that sometimes the words I say can cause her to doubt herself, so Father, help me to watch my tongue and speak encouraging words to her, even when I've had a difficult day. I thank You for this amazing woman. She is such a blessing to me. I pray that today and every day she can receive Your truth over all the areas of her heart. Amen.

The thing she needs most is hearing how valuable she is to you and to her Creator.

love in action . . .

Together: Choose a Scripture passage that reminds you of your value in Christ. When difficulties arise, read it to each other.

For her: The next time your wife faces a difficult season, pull her close, tell her she is loved, read an encouraging Scripture, and listen to her heart.

WEEK

4

SCALING THE HEIGHTS

A prayer for overcoming fear with faith

Don't be afraid, for I am with you. Don't be discouraged, for I am your God. I will strengthen you and help you. I will hold you up with my victorious right hand.

ISAIAH 41:10

One of our most cherished memories involves overcoming our shared fear of heights. It happened during a challenging hike at Angels Landing in Utah's Zion National Park The trail had always intrigued us, but the thought of navigating a narrow path with a one-thousand-foot drop on either side, secured only by a cable, was daunting.

We made a pact before the hike: we would go at our own pace, support each other through every anxious moment, and agree that if either of us wanted to turn back, we would. With this understanding, we faced our fears head-on.

We caught the bus to the trailhead, said a prayer, and began our ascent. As we reached the cable section, an unexpected peace settled over us. Knowing we had to be brave for each other and trusting that God was with us made all the difference. Reaching the top was exhilarating. The views were incredible, like a slice of heaven on earth.

This experience mirrors how we deal with fear in marriage. At times we face insurmountable challenges, with risks and dangers that paralyze us. But when we unite as a couple, with the assurance of God's protection and each other's support, our fears become more manageable. That mutual reliance and trust make the journey a lot easier.

Heavenly Father, I lift up my wife to You, asking that You soothe any anxieties and replace her fears with Your peace. *Gently remind her of the countless blessings that surround her. Grant her the ability to see Your goodness in every situation, turning fear into a steadfast trust in You.*

Father, empower me to be a pillar of support for her through prayer, service, encouragement, and simply being there. As she navigates trials, let her feel Your presence and my unwavering support, knowing she is not alone. My wife capably handles so many of life's hurdles, but I pray that she doesn't rely solely on her own strength. May she lean on You, trusting in Your ability to uplift and sustain her.

Your Word tells us that perfect love casts out fear. I pray that Your perfect love would envelop her, extinguishing any sparks of fear, and that she would find comfort and strength in Your truths. You are our loving Father, and I am endlessly thankful for the gift of my wife. Please grant her peace today and in all the days to come. Amen.

When we face fear in our lives, we can stand securely on the foundation of God's love.

love in action . . .

Together: Set a game plan for facing overwhelming fears head-on. Commit to being there for each other, no matter what.

—— • ——

For her: If your wife is facing fears, let her know you care and look for ways to help her find peace.

WEEK

5

OVERCOMING DISCOURAGEMENT

A prayer for strength to persevere

That is why we never give up. Though our bodies are dying, our spirits are being renewed every day.

2 CORINTHIANS 4:16

A few years into our marriage, Stefanie began to feel a call from God to do online ministry. At the time, we were both still teaching at the Christian school in California, and we had no concept of what such a ministry entailed, especially on social media. Once she decided to pursue this calling, we both committed to going all in and doing whatever it took to spread the gospel online. We learned everything we could about it.

In the process, we have often faced great opposition or difficulty. In those moments that Stefanie is feeling discouraged, I have the opportunity to point her back to God and be strong for her through words of affirmation, kindness, and gentleness.

To be honest, I've failed at this many times, but each failure has taught me how to improve moving forward. I've learned to listen to Stefanie's needs, assure her of my support, and show her where to find the strength she needs to persevere in her calling. I can't do it on my own, but God gives me the grace to be strong for her when challenges arise.

Being courageous for our wives and helping them to keep going starts by understanding where our strength comes from. Any time we try to support them in our own strength, we are on shaky ground. But with God, we have a foundation that cannot be shaken.

Heavenly Father, I pray for my wife. *I pray that You would strengthen her today. Give her peace and hope for the amazing future that You have for her. I pray that You would encourage her in her talents and abilities and in the ways that she loves other people. Help her to persevere in the areas that she feels weak, worried, or discouraged, and encourage her with Your words of love and truth.*

I pray that You will reinforce her in areas of weakness, with truth based on Your Word. Secure her in Your arms of love, and allow me to find ways to support her throughout the day. Strengthen me to be a good husband to her. Help me to have patience and be gentle with her. Teach me how to build her up with encouraging words, and let my actions show the safety she has in our marriage. Protect her today. I pray that we would grow closer together as we grow close to You. Amen.

You cannot help her grow stronger by doing it in your own strength.

love in action . . .

Together: Resolve to take time to pray for each other when a difficult situation arises in your marriage.

—— • ——

For her: When your wife faces difficulties, turn to God for the strength to support her.

WEEK

6

WATCHING OUR TONE

A prayer for graciousness in speech

Always be humble and gentle. Be patient with each other, making allowance for each other's faults because of your love.

EPHESIANS 4:2

One of the hardest things for me to learn in our marriage has been to take care in the tone of voice I use in conversation. When we were dating, I was trying to woo Stefanie, so I was extremely gentle and gracious in my speech.

After we got married, I quickly realized that the way I was communicating in daily life was not landing quite the way I wanted it to. A simple "yeah, I can make dinner" could be taken different ways depending on my tone.

Often, our voice reflects our mood or the situation. After a long day in the classroom, I might say I would make dinner in a way that seemed passive-aggressive when I was really just agreeing to prepare our meal. Some of the biggest mix-ups come from how we sound to our spouses.

If you said the same thing to your brother or your neighbor, they might not think anything of it. But to your wife, it can come across in a completely different way. Once I realized this, I began speaking more gently, using a softer tone. And sure enough, this has saved us from many an argument.

That's not to say that conversation issues are one-sided. Stefanie has learned to be more gracious with me as well. We both play a role and need to daily ask God for grace and humility in how we speak to each other. As we consider how our words impact the other person, we will ensure a strong relationship.

Dear God, I pray that You would guide my wife and me in our conversations with each other. *Teach us to be humble, caring, and gentle. Show us how to be patient, slow to speak, and slow to become angry. When things come up that are upsetting, I pray that we would take time to calm down and talk. May we treat each other the way we would want to be treated, and may we always give each other the benefit of the doubt.*

My wife is my best friend, and I desire to make her feel special. Show me how to care for her needs and sacrificially love her like Jesus did for me. I pray that You would give me the grace to be gentle in my speech and my actions with her. Allow me to communicate my feelings to her in a way she can receive. And give her the grace to receive my words as intended. Show her the ways that I need her to speak to me to get through to my heart. I pray for protection from any schemes of the enemy who seeks to divide us. I pray we love each other more each day for the rest of our lives. Amen.

The more gently you speak to your wife, the more you'll unlock her heart.

love in action . . .

Together: Agree upon a way to gently remind each other when you are using the wrong tone of voice.

—— • ——

For her: Seek to use a gentle tone in all conversations with your wife.

WEEK

7

TIME FOR A RESET

A prayer for capacity to fulfill her responsibilities

Two people are better off than one,
for they can help each other succeed.

ECCLESIASTES 4:9

Stefanie and I both have high-capacity jobs, requiring us to perform at a high level in order to be successful in our business together. As entrepreneurs, we often face challenges in which our responsibilities far outweigh our capacity. There have been a few times when Stefanie or I have felt extremely overwhelmed and needed a break to rejuvenate, rest, and be prepared to perform again.

We always turn first to God, laying our burdens at His feet and asking for the strength and energy we need for each task. But a little encouragement and support from others never hurts. Whenever Stefanie talks about being overwhelmed, I have found that pulling her aside and finding a way to connect with her—whether that's giving her a massage or putting our phones down and having a conversation about something funny—gives us the reset we need. We can regain perspective, then identify what needs to be done, get it done together, and set aside time soon for rest.

I have also found success in taking tasks off her plate, expressing a desire to spend time with her, or encouraging her to take the break she needs. Then we both consider how we can plan better for the future—being intentional about taking on tasks that fill us up rather than pour us out.

Dear God, I lift up my wife to You, asking that You would expand her capacity today. *She juggles so many responsibilities, and I know that she can feel pulled in many different directions. I pray for clarity on which tasks need to get done and which tasks can wait. Grant her peace over the anxieties that come with having so much on her plate.*

My wife is a very capable person, and I am so thankful for all that she does for me and our family each day. Give me eyes to notice all she does, and help me to encourage her in ways that would speak life, hope, and strength over her. Give me wisdom about how I can take a burden off of her. I pray that we will take moments away to gain peace and purpose over the many things we have going on right now. Allow us to cast our burdens on You and to know that You will care for us as we move forward together. Amen.

Our capacity is expanded when we choose to lay our burdens at the feet of Christ.

love in action . . .

Together: Set aside some time without distractions. Take deep breaths and talk, then strategize how to lessen each other's load.

For her: Find ways to take a burden off of your wife this week, and set aside time for her to relax.

Father,
grant my wife
the ability to see
Your goodness
in every situation,
turning fear into
steadfast trust
in You.

WEEK

8

CHOOSING WISELY

A prayer for God's guidance in decisions

If any of you lacks wisdom, let him ask God, who gives generously to all without reproach, and it will be given him.

JAMES 1:5, ESV

Have you ever had trouble making a decision? We were once presented with major opportunities that at the time would have been game changers for us and for our business.

We talked about them together and were so excited about the financial opportunity. Our involvement would undoubtedly have put us on the map. But we couldn't shake the feeling of unrest. Neither of us had peace.

After much prayer and seeking God, Stefanie hinted that we needed to say no to these opportunities. I reluctantly agreed, and we declined. Just a couple of months later, we learned that each and every one of those opportunities had fallen through because of the global pandemic. Our peers who had said yes lost out on money and time they had put toward those efforts.

Trusting God with our decisions and allowing His wisdom to replace momentary success ultimately blessed our marriage, our business, and our lives.

Dear God, I pray that You would pour out Your wisdom over my wife's decisions. *Give her discernment over the choices she has to make this week. It says in Your Word that when we seek wisdom, You offer it generously. I pray that You would prompt her to seek You first each day, and that she would find life and truth in Your Word. Guide her thoughts, her choices, and her actions, that she may walk in Your path and fulfill Your purpose for her life. Equip her with the wisdom to make choices that honor You, choices that are aligned with Your will and Your Word.*

Show me how to support her each day, and give me the wisdom to guide her in the right direction. Help me to encourage and uplift her to continue to grow in the purpose You have for her. Protect our marriage from outside voices or influences that are not aligned with Your truth and want to get in the way of Your call. In the name of Jesus, amen.

God has all the wisdom we need to make decisions together. All we have to do is ask for it.

love in action . . .

Together: Talk through some of the decisions you have to make, and pray over each of them, asking God for wisdom.

—•—

For her: Tell your wife how she has blessed your family by a decision she made recently. Thank her for trusting God through that decision.

WEEK

9

ACCENTUATE THE POSITIVE

A prayer for encouragement

Pleasant words are like a honeycomb, sweetness to the soul and health to the bones.

PROVERBS 16:24, NKJV

One of the best ways that I have found for being intentional about my relationship with Stefanie is through words of encouragement. Each day I try to write her a note and place it on her desk before we start work.

So often, the timing of my note brings her laughter, joy, or tears, leading to moments of peace, connection, and greater intimacy. I do this as I am completing my Bible study for the day, offering her a Scripture or a word of encouragement. Those notes let her know that I am thinking about her and that I appreciate all she does.

Like anything, it takes time to build a habit. I keep sticky notes on my desk so I will remember to write a few words before I get up. I thank her for something she did that meant a lot to me, or I'll say sorry for something I did that hurt her. Sometimes it's just a simple "I love you, and I am so proud of you." That's all it takes.

There's an old saying that it's the thought that counts, and when it comes to encouraging your wife, the thought and the action go a long way to make her feel loved. Whatever approach you take, I hope you'll find a way to consistently communicate to your wife how much you appreciate her.

Heavenly Father, I pray that my wife is encouraged this week through her interactions with You, me, and others. *Show her the blessings in her life, and allow her to receive the encouragement others give her each day. Help her to know that her worth is not based on anything she does but only on the fact that she is Your child, beautifully and wonderfully made.*

Father, I find that as I grow closer to You, I become a much better husband. Give me the strength to be patient, kind, gentle, and humble as I choose to love my wife every single day. I pray I would find ways to encourage her with my words and my actions. Help my treatment of her reflect how much I love her. Show us ways to be an encouragement to each other, and help us be intentional with the ways we show it. I pray that our marriage would inspire others to encourage each other more in their marriages. Help our marriage to thrive in this season and in the next. Amen.

A daily word of encouragement can bring joy and peace to your home.

love in action . . .

Together: Foster an environment of appreciation by making a point of saying five encouraging things to each other each day.

—— • ——

For her: Write a note to your wife listing five things you love about her. Highlight the ways she is a blessing to you.

WEEK
10

PRIORITIZING FRIENDSHIPS

A prayer for supportive relationships

As iron sharpens iron, so a friend sharpens a friend.
PROVERBS 27:17

Navigating friendships within the context of marriage can be challenging. However, I've discovered that it is invaluable for each of us to have loving and supportive friends. From the outset of our marriage, we prioritized nurturing positive friendships for each other. This often meant making individual sacrifices to ensure we both had a supportive community.

For a significant portion of our marriage, we shared a single car. I remember frequently driving Stefanie to meet her friends, finding a nearby place to park, and then being there to pick her up afterward. Even when it was not the most convenient for me, I made it a clear priority, demonstrating the importance I placed on Stefanie having these friendships. We consistently scheduled these get-togethers, making every effort to accommodate them.

What we learned through this journey was the power of intentionality. It may not always have been easy or convenient to foster each other's friendships, but being deliberate about it proved to be a key ingredient for enriching our marriage. It's a practice that continues to bring vitality and depth to our relationship.

Heavenly Father, today I bring my wife's friendships before You. *I pray that You will guide incredible people into her life, friends who will offer support, uplift her spirit, draw her closer to You, and uphold the sanctity of our marriage.*

I ask that these friends be ones who avoid gossip and negative talk, especially about their spouses. Instead, may they be women who unite in prayer, supporting and encouraging each other in their marital journeys. Father, bless her with companions who will walk alongside her through all of life's ups and downs, being present in times of need and leaning on her when they face challenges.

I pray that my wife's time with friends replenishes her, filling her with peace and joy that she can bring back into our marriage. Guide her in nurturing new friendships and restoring past ones that will enrich this season of her life. May she find dependable and loving friends, reflective of the love and care she so freely gives.

Thank you, Lord, for blessing me with a life partner who is also my best friend. I trust in Your provision for meaningful and lasting friendships in her life, now and in the future. Amen.

Prioritizing friendships will bring enrichment and support to your marriage.

love in action . . .

Together: Plan ways for each of you to spend time with friends this week. To find new friends, consider joining a church small group.

—•—

For her: Watch for ways you can prioritize your wife's time with her friends this week.

WEEK

11

MONEY MATTERS

A prayer for peace over finances

Don't worry about these things, saying, "What will we eat? What will we drink? What will we wear?" These things dominate the thoughts of unbelievers, but your heavenly Father already knows all your needs.

MATTHEW 6:31-32

Conversations and arguments about money are a common experience in marriage, and they're certainly something we've encountered in our own journey. There have been numerous occasions when our resources were limited, requiring us to trust deeply in God. In these moments, we always faced a choice: to point fingers at each other in blame or join hands in prayer.

A source of comfort during times of financial strain has been the reminder above from Matthew 6. This passage reassures us that God is aware of our needs and will provide for us as necessary. Fixating on what we lack or worrying excessively about the future can cause us to miss the blessings of the present. The message is clear: God provides enough for each day. Sometimes it may be more, but it is never less. He faithfully meets our daily needs as we trust in Him and diligently pursue the tasks He has set before us.

Over the years, God's provision has been evident more times than we can count, even in moments when it seemed all was lost. When financial stress threatens the peace of your marriage, I encourage you to turn toward each other. Offer apologies and forgiveness as needed. Then, turn together to God, allowing Him to fulfill your needs. His consistent faithfulness has been a beacon of hope in our lives, and I am confident it can be in yours as well.

Heavenly Father, I acknowledge that financial matters can be a source of stress, leading to conflict and disagreements in our marriage. *I pray that in such times, You will become the binding force in our relationship. May we turn to You, seeking Your guidance and peace, rather than succumbing to blame.*

Help us to rely on You as our Provider, embracing the truth that You supply our daily needs. At the same time, I seek Your wisdom in managing our finances and pray for mentors who can guide us to use our resources wisely and to steward Your blessings responsibly. Guide us in formulating strategies that enhance our financial well-being. I pray for opportunities to be generous with what we have, trusting that as we give, You will continue to provide.

You are immensely good to us, Lord. I pray that financial management becomes a strength in our marriage. Maintain clarity and purpose in our communication about finances. May our conversations be anchored in trust, love, and open communication. In times of challenge, may we be anchored in Your hope, working together in unity. Amen.

God is our Provider and gives us enough for each day.

love in action . . .

Together: Set aside time regularly to talk about your finances. Seek ways to grow in this area and build trust.

—•—

For her: If your wife is stressed out about finances, listen to her concerns, then strategize without looking for fault.

Father, I pray
that our marriage
is a safe space for my wife
to share the desires of her heart.
May she feel appreciated
and loved.

SEEN, KNOWN, LOVED

A prayer that she feels understood and valued

O Lord, *you have examined my heart and know everything about me. You know when I sit down or stand up. You know my thoughts even when I'm far away. You see me when I travel and when I rest at home. You know everything I do.*

PSALM 139:1-3

Marriage really shines when you feel truly seen, known, and loved by your spouse. This is deeply valued, especially by our wives. I've always enjoyed picking out gifts for Stefanie; it's my way of showing her I'm in tune with what she likes and needs. Seeing her smile as she unwraps a gift I've chosen is one of those little joys in life.

But let's be honest, sometimes I miss the mark. One Christmas, I thought I had nailed the gift-giving. But I noticed Stefanie looked a bit down. I couldn't figure it out. When I asked, she reminded me that she'd been dropping hints about wanting the complete *Full House* DVD set. I face-palmed—how could I forget? I hopped online and ordered it right away, but the moment for a Christmas morning surprise was gone.

She said my oversight wasn't a big deal, but it was a wake-up call for me. I learned the importance of really listening, being fully present. I don't want to just hear Stefanie. I want to understand what she's saying, what she's not saying, and what she truly wants—especially for more important issues than gift-giving. Showing her that I value what she cares about, that I'm paying attention and putting in the effort—that's what makes her feel loved.

Heavenly Father, show me the ways my wife desires to be seen in our everyday interactions. *Give me ears to be attentive to her words, desires, and wishes in our conversations. Help me give her the gift of my presence and attention when we are together so she doesn't feel left out or less important than what I am doing.*

I pray that our marriage is a safe space for her to share the desires of her heart and that I can be gracious and careful with what she shares. May she feel appreciated for what she does and loved for just being her.

I pray for moments where we can laugh, cry, hope, pray, and dream together for the future. Help me to always show her through my actions, my words, and my time that she is valuable to me and that what she cares about is important.

I pray that she gets her worth and value from You alone and that I can always point her back to You when she is discouraged. Open her heart to Your words of truth and allow her to receive my love. I pray she always feels seen, known, and loved. Amen.

Your presence—physically, mentally, emotionally, and spiritually—is essential for your wife to feel seen, known, and loved.

love in action . . .

Together: Ask your wife if there is anything she has been trying to tell you that you have not picked up on. Try to follow through with what she communicates.

—•—

For her: Spend time with your wife, being intentionally present with no distractions.

WEEK

13

WHEN ENOUGH IS ENOUGH

A prayer for contentment

I have learned how to be content with whatever I have. I know how to live on almost nothing or with everything. I have learned the secret of living in every situation, whether it is with a full stomach or empty, with plenty or little.

PHILIPPIANS 4:11-12

Recently, Stefanie and I saw that a large pet store was going out of business. They had sales of up to 80 percent off. We had actually wanted to get a couple of things for our fish, and because we also have a Pomeranian and a new kitty, we decided to see what was left.

Prices were seemingly slashed to the bone, and we had soon filled a shopping cart. As we headed for the checkout, Stefanie stopped me and asked if she could look up the items online to make sure we were getting a good deal. We soon realized the prices weren't much different from what we usually pay, so I dropped the cat food and cat litter back on the shelf. I'll never forget the way Stefanie tossed this little bag of fish food on top of the pile and walked away—as if we had conquered the temptation for more, right then and there.

Later, we were happy that we had walked out of there, content with what we already had and thankful for our blessings.

With the constant pull around us to get more and more—the new Ford, the updated iPhone—it's important to remind ourselves that all we really need at the end of the day is each other and God, and He will supply anything else.

Heavenly Father, I pray for a spirit of contentment in our marriage and in my wife's heart. *Lord, You are the fountain of all joy, and You've faithfully provided for every one of our needs. May Your love and peace envelop my wife as she goes about her day. Keep her from the trap of comparison, which only serves to steal joy. Instead, let her keep her eyes steadfastly on You.*

Guide my wife to turn to You in moments of longing or dissatisfaction. Gently lead her away from anything that might disrupt her peace or happiness. When we're tempted to yearn for more, help us to come together in conversation and seek Your wisdom. I pray that our marriage remains free from jealousy or envy, whether toward each other or those around us. Help us both to recognize and appreciate the blessings in our home, our relationship, and our lives, cultivating a sense of thankfulness and contentment.

I pray for deeper connection and peace as we bring our desires, dreams, and aspirations before You. I place my trust in You for my wife's well-being and our future. You provide all we need, and so much more. Amen.

Gratitude brings more joy than anything money can buy.

love in action . . .

Together: Write down three things you thank God for and three things you are thankful for about each other.

—— • ——

For her: Tell your wife that you are happy and content in your marriage. This is an incredible gift, letting her know she is more than enough.

WEEK

14

NO MORE EXCUSES

A prayer that she would hold firm to God's truth

Jesus said . . . "You are truly my disciples if you remain faithful to my teachings. And you will know the truth, and the truth will set you free."

JOHN 8:31-32

I'll be honest: there was a time when I was pretty bad about reading my Bible. I had all sorts of excuses—too busy, simply forgot—all while wondering why I wasn't experiencing much joy. Having grown up in the church, I figured I already knew what the Bible had to say, so why bother reading it regularly? It was a rough period, and stubbornly, I wasn't keen on changing my ways.

Then, I married a woman who turns to God's Word for everything—hope, joy, guidance, wisdom. This difference in our approaches soon became a glaring issue. I had to decide whether to continue making excuses or to make Bible reading a priority. Fortunately, I chose the latter.

The transformation was remarkable. I became happier, more grateful, and even more successful. But the biggest change was in our marriage. Now, when we face tough times, it is no longer just Stefanie who draws us back to God's truth. When she feels low, I can help her stand firm too.

Taking time each day to immerse yourself in God's Word is invaluable. It provides the wisdom needed to support your wife and strengthen your marriage. This practice has been a lifesaver for my marriage. I truly believe it can make a significant difference for you too.

Heavenly Father, I am deeply grateful for the easy access we have to Your Word. *The ability to dive into Your teachings at any moment is an incredible blessing, one that many don't have. Today, my heart is with my wife. In moments of difficulty or discouragement, I pray that she finds peace and strength in Your truth. Remind her, Lord, that Your Word is a lamp for her feet and a light on her path, guiding her through every decision and challenge.*

I ask for the wisdom to always lead her back to Your truth. In times when we find ourselves without ground to stand on, let Your words of love, hope, vision, and peace be our firm foundation. In a world clamoring for our attention, where so many things tempt us to seek our worth elsewhere, grant us the clarity to see through the deceptions.

Strengthen my wife in her moments of weakness, and uplift her with encouraging words. Inspire me to be her supporter and confidant, especially when times get tough. May our first instinct always be to turn to You for help and direction in the face of trials. You are our loving Father, and we trust in Your guidance for our lives and our marriage. Amen.

Let God's Word be the truth you stand on when times get tough.

love in action . . .

Together: Make it a habit to read your Bibles as a couple. This will give you a solid foundation no matter what you face.

—— • ——

For her: The next time your wife is facing something difficult, listen first, pray for her, and hold tightly to the Word of God for guidance.

WEEK

15

REAL-WORLD CHAMPION

A prayer for self-control

A person without self-control is like a city with broken-down walls.
PROVERBS 25:28

Self-control is an area I have had to grow in. I get really into hobbies, sports, or activities and want to be the best at them. Let's just say I can get a little obsessive. This can cause problems because I sometimes forget to do more important things.

I used to spend hours playing video games after work. With my online friends, I'd conquer raids, take down epic bosses, and be the champion of a virtual world. But I was less and less the champion of my wife's world. I was letting her down, and something needed to change.

I took inventory of why I liked those games so much, then started exercising self-control over my playing. After Stefanie had spent a long day at work, she just wanted to feel special in spending time with me. That was not a night to play video games for three hours.

As I set boundaries, became aware of the impact of my actions, and exercised self-control, I felt more like a champion in real life, and I felt more fulfilled. Rather than running off to a fantasy world, I was living my dream life in reality. When I do play games now, I feel free to enjoy them fully during the time I set apart for them.

When we choose our priorities, put up strong boundaries, and exercise self-control, it brings peace to our marriage.

Heavenly Father, today, I specifically pray for self-control in our marriage. *I pray for my wife to exercise self-control in her habits, routines, hobbies, interactions, communication, and her health. I pray that I can encourage her to use her gifts and abilities for Your good, and to bless our marriage. I ask that You would break any strongholds in her life that are holding her back or causing her to act out in ways she shouldn't. Help her to go to You first with any problems, worries, or concerns. I submit her mental health into Your hands, and I ask that her worth and value would not come from anything other than You. Help her to choose pursuits that bring her life, hope, and peace. I pray that self-control is a pillar of strength in our marriage. Father, help me to never take her for granted and to always point her back to You. You are such a good Father. Amen.*

Self-control allows you to unlock freedom over any strongholds in your life and marriage.

love in action . . .

Together: Talk about the ways you see each other showing self-control. Create a plan together to encourage growth in this area.

For her: Encourage your wife in the ways she is exercising self-control. Watch for ways to build her up.

FOLLOW THOSE DREAMS

A prayer for confidence

Let us think of ways to motivate one another to acts of love and good works. And . . . encourage one another, especially now that the day of his return is drawing near.

HEBREWS 10:24-25

One of my biggest desires is that Stefanie would feel like she can conquer anything she wants to. I pray she never feels like I doubt her abilities or wouldn't have her back in whatever God calls her to do.

Early in our marriage, after we had both worked at the Christian school in California for three years, Stefanie felt a stirring in her heart to work online sharing the gospel and helping people with their relationships, specifically through social media. I knew nothing about social media at that time, but I knew Stefanie had a great story to tell. If God was calling her to this, I didn't want to stand in the way.

But I was at a crossroads: Would I expect her to find another job to keep bringing in a paycheck while pursuing this mission? Or would I support her fully to boost her confidence and start her off in the best way possible? I chose the latter. We took the money we had been saving for a trip to Europe and put it toward this new venture. I didn't want her to doubt for one second that I would support her fully. This gave her the confidence to walk into her new dream, and that leap of faith changed our lives.

Heavenly Father, I thank You for my wife's talents, abilities, and passions. *You have created her so wonderfully. I pray today that she would feel how much You love her. Father, my wife will thrive when she feels confident and encouraged in her relationship with You and with me. Please encourage her today, whether it's through a random text from a friend, an encouraging word from a stranger, or a loving gesture from a family member. Help her to feel confident and hopeful about her future.*

My wife is an incredible blessing to me. Prompt me to encourage her in a way she needs encouragement, give me the resources to support her dreams and ambitions, and show me how to love her in the way that will most bless her. I believe in my wife, and I want her to achieve every dream. Bind the enemy who wants her to compare or be jealous of anyone else, and show her the amazing plans You have for her life. I thank You for Your incredible kindness to us. Amen.

A woman who is confident is clothed with strength and dignity. She trusts the plans God has for her.

love in action . . .

Together: Write down three things you want to accomplish together. Check in with each other to see how close you are to accomplishing those dreams.

—•—

For her: Seek one thing you can do to move your wife toward a dream she has. Show her that you support her unconditionally.

WEEK

17

ALL IN THE FAMILY

A prayer for positive in-law relationships

All of you should be of one mind. Sympathize with each other. Love each other as brothers and sisters. Be tenderhearted, and keep a humble attitude.

1 PETER 3:8

One of the scariest moments can be meeting the family of our significant other. Stefanie met my family before we even started dating when she came over with friends to watch a movie. My parents knew I had a crush on her, and they were ecstatic about meeting her. After we started dating, we planned a trip for me to meet Stefanie's parents. Let's just say, it was memorable.

Stefanie left a few days before me, and I flew out to join her for Christmas, meeting her dad and mom, along with her sister and her sister's boyfriend. After exchanging pleasantries, I excused myself to use the bathroom.

And of course, I clogged the toilet.

To my horror, I could not find a plunger, so I asked Stefanie if she knew where it was. She didn't, so she quietly asked her sister. Her sister, bless her heart, yelled, "DAD! Caleb clogged the toilet. Where's the plunger?"

I was stunned, but her dad found the plunger and went to fix the problem. I pleaded with him to let me do it, but he wasn't having it.

Thankfully, the rest of that trip went well, and we are now married, so maybe it wasn't too bad. But in-law relationships can be tricky. Having a unified front and being honest about how we feel helps us navigate those relationships.

Heavenly Father, I choose today to lift up our in-law relations. *I know that being with my family can be a blessing but can also be a cause of stress for my wife, so please give her peace and understanding with my family. Help her to be kind in talking about them, as well as in her interactions with them. I pray that she would feel comfortable to share situations that have hurt her. Reveal to her any issues with her family or mine, and convict her heart to make a change where needed and to communicate with me about it.*

Father, help us both to leave our families and cling to each other. Give us wisdom to communicate in ways that would honor each other's family and not cause division. Give us grace with each other, and show us ways to pursue unity and build each other up. May we both make efforts to love on each other's families and help each other feel more loved in the process. Give us peace and hope for the future together and with our in-laws. Amen.

Having a united front and grace-filled conversations will help you navigate in-law relationships.

love in action . . .

Together: Make sure you are unified as a couple before including in-laws. Agree to talk before making decisions and to not inappropriately include family.

—•—

For her: Invest in relationships with your wife's family. Support her in dealing with her family or yours.

Father,
protect my wife
from worry or fear.
May Your truth
be the foundation
she stands on
in trials.

WEEK

18

LIVING IN THE MOMENT

A prayer for freedom from worry

Whoever dwells in the shelter of the Most High
will rest in the shadow of the Almighty.

PSALM 91:1, NIV®

Throughout the lockdown in 2020, Stefanie, like many others, wasn't able to see her family. No holidays, no Christmas, nothing. At the time, we lived close to my family, so we got to see them. But for Stefanie, it was a difficult season.

After praying and talking about it, we decided to drive across the country for a visit. That's over three thousand miles, one way. While we could usually control who we came into contact with, there were still many unknowns. We both had so much anxiety about the trip.

As we set out in our 2005 Suburban, with 280,000 miles on it, God brought to mind Psalm 91, a prayer of protection, and we began to speak those words over and over as we drove. With each mile, we felt our anxieties falling off. We could sense God's presence, and we knew that we didn't have to worry.

We eventually made it to Pennsylvania and had a wonderful time—and I learned a valuable lesson: we aren't promised anything other than the present moment. Worry doesn't help and certainly won't add to your life. I learned to put my fears in God's hands, trusting Him to protect me, and then to make the most of the time I have. Doing so brings peace and hope to our marriage, as Stefanie's worries fade away too.

Heavenly Father, I pray for the worries, anxieties, and fears that my wife experiences throughout the day. *I ask that You would grant her peace over all of it. Draw near to her as she draws near to You. Worrying doesn't add a single hour to her life, so I ask that You would guide my wife into prayer before she starts worrying. Lead me to be proactive in prayer, too, and attuned to her needs so that I can help her find peace.*

Protect my wife from any thoughts that would cause her to worry or fear, and help her to dwell on truths that would draw her closer to You. I pray that I would be a support to her and encourage her daily and that I would remind her of the blessings around her. Father, I know that when we draw close to You, we feel more at peace, so help me to be a leader in that way. Show me how to pray for my wife so she will experience peace and joy. I pray that Your words of truth would be the foundation we can stand on whenever we face trials. You are our good and loving Father. Amen.

Worrying doesn't add a single hour to your life, but choosing God's peace allows you to enjoy every moment.

love in action . . .

Together: When worries come up, pray Psalm 91 together. Allow God's peace to cover you, and choose to live in the moment.

—•—

For her: If your wife experiences worry this week, pray for her and speak words of hope and life over your future.

WEEK

19

SPARKING THE FLAME

A prayer for fostering intimacy

Let your wife be a fountain of blessing for you. Rejoice in the wife of your youth. She is a loving deer, a graceful doe. Let her breasts satisfy you always. May you always be captivated by her love.

PROVERBS 5:18-19

When it comes to romance, the movies portray an environment where both of you are always "ready." But true romance takes effort. It's often the thoughtful and intentional acts that turn a spark into a flame.

Speaking of flames, one year I planned a perfect evening: a nice dinner, a favorite movie, and some time for intimacy with each other. I thought, *This night is going to be amazing*. When it was time for our movie, I lit the tiki torches on the porch and went back in to grab drinks.

Suddenly, things got brighter in the house, and I turned around to utter horror. One of the torches had fallen over onto the outdoor furniture, and there was a flame almost six feet high. In a panic, I rushed for a bucket of water.

Meanwhile, Stefanie flew out the front door in search of one of the apartment complex fire extinguishers. I heard a loud *BANG* and the crash of broken glass, and she ran back in with an extinguisher. She gave it to me, and we put out the fire.

"Well, that wasn't the way I thought tonight would go," I said.

Regardless, Stefanie has always appreciated my efforts to cultivate romance. While I might crash and burn at times, other times I knock it out of the park. Intimacy isn't perfect like the movies. But it's far better when we make it a priority.

Heavenly Father, I am so grateful to have someone I can be one with and share deep levels of intimacy with. *Thank You for her body, each part masterfully created by You. In those intimate moments, help us to be unselfish and gentle, listening and learning each other's needs and desires.*

Teach me ways to create an atmosphere of romance that would cultivate physical intimacy with my wife. I know that when she feels appreciated and loved, she has more of a desire for sex, so help me to love on her in the ways she needs. I pray that we can continue to grow in this area of our marriage over time and have open communication about the ways we can love each other better. Protect our intimacy. The enemy seeks to destroy marriages, and he would love to infiltrate our marriage bed. Help us to stay pure before You and each other. Protect our eyes and hearts from anything that would lead us astray. Help me to always delight in my wife and pursue her all the days of my life. Amen.

When two become one, it is one of the greatest expressions of God's love for us in marriage.

love in action . . .

Together: Set aside time this week to do something romantic together. Ask your wife what would make her feel special.

—•—

For her: Cultivate romance in your marriage: a candlelit dinner, a sweet note or text, a date together, or something unexpected.

WEEK

20

HEALTHY FRIENDSHIPS

A prayer that she would guard her heart and mind

Guard your heart above all else, for it determines the course of your life.

PROVERBS 4:23

Stefanie and I have both had friends who caused us to doubt and question ourselves. I'm not talking about healthy accountability. I'm talking about people who make you feel bad for being you.

Stefanie always makes me feel like I can be fully me, and I make it my utmost priority to protect her heart so she can feel the same way. She had one friendship that always left her deflated. She would come home feeling bad that we had such a positive relationship with each other.

After asking God for wisdom about protecting her heart, I began to ask Stefanie questions and suggested that she pray about whether this was a friendship she should keep. If it was not bringing her closer to God, helping her marriage, and growing her as an individual, then it might not be the best relationship.

She later came to me saying she didn't want to be friends with this woman anymore. Since making that decision, she has felt more free to be herself in our marriage and in her life.

The conversation about that friendship wasn't easy, but it was a tangible way I could help protect her heart. Our wives' friendships can be tricky to navigate, so seeking God's counsel is important. It's best not to overreact. Instead submit it to God and He will give you discernment for approaching the conversation with grace and humility.

Heavenly Father, I pray that You would protect my wife's heart. *Keep anything away that would cause her to question her worth or value in You, and fill her with peace, joy, and confidence. Help her to have discernment about her friendships and relationships. What we allow into our hearts flows through us and out from us. As my wife goes through her day, I pray that she makes spending time in Your Word a priority, that she is careful with who she listens to and what content she consumes. I ask that You would bring positive friendships, mentors, and community into her life to help her thrive.*

Father, my wife's heart is precious to me, so please help me be intentional about taking care of her needs, wants, and desires. Show me how to proactively pursue her in ways that make her feel loved. I pray that You would protect her heart from anything that is not of You. Help us to cling to Your truths in our marriage. Amen.

Protect your heart, for what you put into it also flows out from it.

love in action . . .

Together: Take inventory together of the voices in your marriage. If anything is taking away from your relationship, make changes to protect your hearts.

—•—

For her: Ask God for wisdom about protecting your wife's heart. Approach conversations with grace and gentleness, and speak the truth in love.

WEEK

21

MARRIAGE KILLER

A prayer for letting go of pride

Dress yourselves in humility as you relate to one another, for "God opposes the proud but gives grace to the humble." So humble yourselves under the mighty power of God, and at the right time he will lift you up in honor.

1 PETER 5:5-6

Pride is the killer of marriages. It keeps us from wanting to listen more, be humble, and accept that we might be at fault. Pride often rears its ugly head during arguments. In those times, we feel most vulnerable and are least likely to humble ourselves.

I have always tried my best to take care of Stefanie and meet her needs. So when she would bring up something that bothered her, I would get extra defensive and offended. I felt like she should overlook my wrongs because of all the rights, especially if I hadn't meant to cause a problem. Pride was at the center of these feelings, and I would only further entrench myself in defensiveness the longer the argument lasted.

Finally, I realized that taking care of her meant setting aside my pride in those moments—listening to her feelings, being willing to consider whether I needed to change my actions, and understanding that her comments didn't mean she no longer loved me or that I hadn't done enough overall. If I truly cared about her, I would be willing to change my response. This goes for both of us, of course. It's okay to be vulnerable with each other, and we benefit far more from listening and being kind than from being hard-hearted and prideful.

Heavenly Father, I pray that You would keep pride from our relationship. *The enemy is the father of pride and the divider of marriages, so I pray that You would bind him in the name of Jesus. Protect our hearts and minds from developing a selfish posture.*

May your humility reign in my wife's heart. Help her to be kind, gentle, and caring with her words and actions. Show her anywhere pride has a stronghold in her heart, and show her how to choose humility in those areas.

Father, together we are one, and we pray that nothing would come into our marriage that would cause division between us. I pray that we would look to You when we have disagreements and that You would restore any broken areas of our life. Give us wisdom and strategies to fight pride together and foster an atmosphere of joy and peace in our home. Gratitude is an amazing weapon against pride, so we choose to be thankful each day for the blessings You have given us. Thank You for Your loving-kindness and for giving me a partner for life. Amen.

Gratitude is the most powerful weapon against pride in your marriage.

love in action . . .

Together: Pick one day that you both will commit to saying nothing negative about each other, no matter what comes up. Release it to God, and be thankful for each other.

—— • ——

For her: Ask God to reveal anything you are holding on to against your wife. Apologize to her, and move forward with gratitude and humility.

WEEK

22

PACKING UP

A prayer for wisdom in life transitions

Forget all that—it is nothing compared to what I am going to do. For I am about to do something new. See, I have already begun! Do you not see it? I will make a pathway through the wilderness. I will create rivers in the dry wasteland.

ISAIAH 43:18-19

A few years ago, Stefanie and I felt a call from God to uproot our lives in Southern California and move across the country to Pittsburgh. Why Pittsburgh? Stefanie was born and raised there, and it is where most of her family lives. Since our business can function from anywhere, we thought that it could work.

We had several confirmations from God, including our current home, which seemed to drop into our laps at an affordable price during a nationwide price hike. At the same time, we were offered our first book deal, which paid for the move. God was behind us in this move, and we knew it.

The hard part was leaving our home in Pasadena. I have never lived anywhere other than California, so this was a big transition for me. But we packed up and set off for the Northeast.

Transitions are part of life, and we have encountered many that have been difficult and unexpected. We've changed careers, lost out on dreams, and experienced a miscarriage of our twin miracle boys. But in each new uncertainty, one thing remained the same: God's truth and the fact that His promises never fail. As we continue to encounter new transitions, we trust that what He sets in motion is, in fact, good. He will finish the work if we are obedient to His leading.

Heavenly Father, I thank You for my wife. *I thank You for the ways that she has been flexible with me in taking on life transitions together. I pray for peace over any looming decisions or changes. Help us to make wise decisions, and allow us to have grace for any mistakes we make along the way. I pray that my wife wouldn't worry about changes but that she would know You have us right where You want us. Reveal to her anything that she needs to fully release into Your hands.*

Help me to support her in any way she needs it—emotionally, physically, or mentally—during life transitions. I pray that I can be gentle with her in our interactions and communicate expectations and changes clearly. Help us to rely on You for our support and foundation, knowing that You direct our paths. Father, You protect us, and You are our strength no matter what we face. I pray that my wife and I will rely wholeheartedly on Your truth to sustain us through any uncertainty. You are our good Father. Amen.

What God sets in motion He fully intends to finish.

love in action . . .

Together: Pray for wisdom over a transition you are facing, and allow God to give you direction.

—— • ——

For her: Find ways to support your wife during times of change. Lend an ear or a helping hand and point her back to God.

WEEK

23

MENTORS

A prayer for wise mentors

Get all the advice and instruction you can,
so you will be wise the rest of your life.
PROVERBS 19:20

There is so much value to be gained from people who have gone before us. Stefanie and I are intentional about seeking positive voices, mentors, and leaders to help guide us. We have taken courses together, attended retreats, and gone through counseling so that we have the best chance of thriving in this important venture—our marriage.

Marriage retreats have been one of our favorite things to do together each year. They are an amazing way for us to connect, get away somewhere new, and learn from experts. For the first few years of our marriage, we attended a retreat at Hume Lake in California. This mountain retreat had breathtaking views, hiking trails, and fun activities to do together. Attending was always a no-brainer.

We have needed those retreats at different seasons of our marriage, but we have gone whether we were thriving or just trying to survive. We've always come home with more hope, better skills, and improved strategies. No matter what season of marriage you are in—newlyweds, seasoned veterans, or in the twilight years of life—taking time to find good mentors and grow together is one of the most valuable things you can do for your marriage.

Heavenly Father, I pray that You would bring us mentors who would bless our marriage, people who would pour into us and speak life and hope into our relationship. *Help us to be proactive in finding people or a church that would encourage us. In difficult seasons or in times we feel alone, help us to pursue mentors and experiences that build intimacy and strengthen our marriage.*

Protect us from anyone who would seek to take away from our marriage or take advantage of us, and guide us toward people who would sharpen us, admonish us, and pray for us as we go through life together. Provide mentors who seek You first and will lead us closer to You.

I pray that I would be a leader in finding support for our marriage. Help me to do it before it's too late. Light a fire in both of us to get the support we need, and guide us always back to Your truth no matter what we face. We thank You for Your love, and for bringing us people who show us Your love daily. Amen.

Find people who speak life, hope, and love into your marriage, bringing you closer to God together.

love in action . . .

Together: Think of ways to spend more time with couples you look up to, and possibly be mentored by them.

—— • ——

For her: Be proactive in finding someone to mentor you as a husband. Share with your wife how this is benefiting you.

WEEK

24

OLD WOUNDS

A prayer for freedom and healing from past pain

Jesus said, "Come to me, all of you who are weary and carry heavy burdens, and I will give you rest. Take my yoke upon you. Let me teach you, because I am humble and gentle at heart, and you will find rest for your souls. For my yoke is easy to bear, and the burden I give you is light."

MATTHEW 11:28-30

Past pain has a way of coming up in marriages from time to time. It makes appearances in arguments or during a movie that triggers emotions.

When Stefanie and I started dating, we both had an immense amount of pain from the past. We had been through heartbreak, abuse, and disappointment. As we talked, we sensed weights falling off our shoulders, just from feeling safe and seen with each other.

One night, I began to tell Stefanie things I had never told anyone. In response, she encouraged me to pray and fully release those wounds to God. Jesus says He wants to give us a light load to carry. We don't have to bear that heavy burden on our own.

That night was a game changer. For the first time in a long time I felt safe. Ever since, I have fought for Stefanie to receive freedom from her past too.

If you and your wife struggle with burdens from the past, I encourage you to seek healing together and separately, no matter how scary it may seem. As those weights begin to fall off, you'll find that living wholeheartedly before God is the best feeling on this earth.

Heavenly Father, I thank You for my wife. *Thank You for protecting her from the things in her past that she might not even have realized were happening. I pray for her complete healing from past pain, trauma, heartbreak, and disappointment. Reveal to me how to pray about the things she is currently dealing with or working through. Show me ways I can help to heal her wounds. Use me to help her grow closer to You and help me to always point her back to You when she is having a hard time.*

Father, I know that certain things can bring up bad memories, so I pray that we can have victory over those past pains. Give us strategies to best set her up for peace in every area of her life. I ask that I can be a part of her healing journey. Show me ways I can do that for her each day. My prayer is that she can live wholeheartedly. Amen.

You were not meant to carry burdens from your past. Release them to God and allow Him to take the weight off your shoulders.

love in action . . .

Together: Commit to talking with each other about any unresolved issues from your past. Seek professional help for any areas that are too difficult to tackle on your own.

—•—

For her: Lift up your wife in prayer each day, asking God to give her peace and freedom from anything holding her back.

WEEK

25

PARTY TIME

A prayer that she feels celebrated

If one part is honored, all the parts are glad.
1 CORINTHIANS 12:26

We have always made celebration a priority in our marriage. There is so much in life that can discourage us. It's important to take time to commemorate our victories.

When Stefanie and I first had the dream of working together to help people in their relationships, marriages, and singleness, we worked nights and weekends to make it come true.

Finally, I was able to retire from teaching and begin working alongside my wife. Stefanie, who has always been great at celebrating me, whether I scored twenty points in a rec league basketball game or got a good opportunity at work, was ecstatic. She really wanted to celebrate this milestone with me, so she threw a huge beach party with family and friends.

So many people came to congratulate us, ask questions about what was next, and pray over us. I felt so honored that she would celebrate me in that way and that so many people would come to show support. It was God's redemption of dead dreams, now being birthed into a lifelong calling.

I am thankful for moments like that because they not only create memories to remember but also allow us to recognize the amazing things that God has done for us.

Heavenly Father, help us to always celebrate one another for the big and small victories. *I pray that my wife would feel safe enough to tell me about accomplishments she is proud of so that I can celebrate them with her. My wife is worth celebrating each day, so please give me the presence of mind to celebrate the things she does for our family and in her work.*

May we foster an environment for celebration in our home. I pray that nothing is too small for us to take time to commemorate together. When we have joyful hearts of celebration, we are happier and healthier people. When my wife feels celebrated and appreciated, she is a happier person and is more giving toward others. Father, You have been so good to us. Please give us more moments to give thanks for and to honor others around us. Amen.

Building an atmosphere of celebration in your home will bring joy, peace, and gratitude to your hearts, inspiring you to do so much more!

love in action . . .

Together: Talk about a big or small victory you could celebrate with family and friends.

—•—

For her: Surprise your wife with a small gift or weekend away to celebrate one of her accomplishments.

Father, prompt me
to pursue my wife
with small and large gestures
that make her feel special.
Keep romance a key
ingredient in our love.

IN THE MOOD

A prayer for romantic connection

Your love delights me, my treasure, my bride. Your love is better than wine, your perfume more fragrant than spices.

SONG OF SONGS 4:10

Cultivating romance in your marriage helps to bring the two of you together and builds intimacy. It doesn't have to take much effort. The intentionality truly matters most. Whether I'm taking time to watch a movie with Stefanie, filling our house with candles, or writing love notes, I have always tried to prioritize doing things that make her feel loved and pursued.

One year, on my birthday, after we had gone to a nice dinner and watched a movie together, we moved on toward the bedroom. Without getting into much detail, we were talking sweetly to each other only to realize that at some point I had butt-dialed my father and recorded our conversation on voicemail. We looked in horror at the counting seconds on the phone. I then had to do something no one wants to do: call my dad and ask him to delete that message without listening to it. Thankfully, I have a trustworthy father.

I hope I have put the fear of God in you to keep your phone in a locked safe during those intimate moments. But while embarrassing, that experience reminds us of the importance of creating an atmosphere where romance is the priority. I hope that it encourages you to do the same. Just turn off your phone first.

Heavenly Father, I pray that romance would be a major part of our marriage and that You would motivate us to make it a priority. *Prompt me with ways that I can pursue my wife throughout the day with small and large gestures that make her feel special. Protect our eyes, hearts, and minds from anything that would hurt our intimacy, and keep us from any temptation that would cause us to go outside of marriage for romance.*

I know that when my wife feels pursued, she feels loved and special, so help me find ways to do that for her each day. Help me let go of pride and choose gentleness and humility in our conversations to cultivate romance.

I pray that my wife would make an effort to romance me in return and love me in ways that would build our intimacy together. Give us hope for the future, and help us to grow in our relationship as we choose You first and each other second. Keep romance a key ingredient in our recipe for love. Amen.

When you are intentional about creating romance, your intimacy will thrive.

love in action . . .

Together: Plan a time to do something romantic together and rekindle the spark in your marriage.

—— • ——

For her: Think of three gestures you know will make your wife feel romanced this week. Carry them out to let her know how special she is.

WEEK

27

IT'S THE SMALL THINGS

A prayer that she will choose acts of kindness

Since God chose you to be the holy people he loves, you must clothe yourselves with tenderhearted mercy, kindness, humility, gentleness, and patience.

COLOSSIANS 3:12

I love doing small things for Stefanie—surprising her with a bouquet of flowers or a little thank-you note. I delight in seeing her smile and in making her feel special. I would never want her to feel like she wasn't important to me. These little acts of kindness show that I am thinking about her and that she is seen and loved.

A while back, I went with my dad and brothers to Kansas City, Missouri. My dad had always dreamed of seeing the Chiefs play at Arrowhead Stadium, so to celebrate his retirement, he flew us all out to see a game together. This, of course, meant that I would be spending a weekend away from Stefanie. I wanted to do something to make her feel special while I was gone, so I bought her a gift and card she could open each day. I was delighted to hear how much she loved each gift.

Little did I know that she had planned the exact same thing for me, hiding gifts in my backpack before I left. I felt so loved as I opened each one. Neither of us did anything crazy elaborate—just small things meant to brighten the other person's day. But I can say from experience, *mission accomplished*!

Heavenly Father, I pray that we would foster an environment together where acts of kindness would be the norm. *Help us to think of big and small ways to make each other feel special throughout the day. I pray this will bring us moments of joy. Help us to be creative, and give us wisdom to do things that would be especially helpful on days we are having a hard time.*

I pray also that I would show my wife how much it means when she is kind and loving to me. May I always appreciate it when she goes out of her way to make me feel respected, loved, and supported. Help us to build consistent habits of gratitude and gentleness so that even on difficult days, we can endure. Thank You for loving us so well. Amen.

Even the smallest act of kindness can make the biggest difference in your wife's day.

love in action . . .

Together: Try a "Kindness Challenge." See how many days you can go with at least one of you doing something kind for the other.

—— • ——

For her: Do something out of the ordinary to be kind to your wife and show her that you appreciate her.

WEEK

28

"TAG—YOU'RE IT!"

A prayer for quality time together

My dove is hiding behind the rocks, behind an outcrop on the cliff. Let me see your face; let me hear your voice. For your voice is pleasant, and your face is lovely.

SONG OF SONGS 2:14

Time is one thing you can't get more of. There's always a chance to make more money, eat more food, or pursue more hobbies, but you can't get back time. That's why Stefanie and I prioritize not just spending time together, but spending quality time together.

Early in our business, we were hired to travel to different US cities to explore the activities they offered. Then we would present the best options for couples to go and enjoy in those locations.

Once, we were at Forest Park in Saint Louis. Forest Park, the site for the 1904 World's Fair, has a zoo, museums, and open spaces. After finishing our work, we headed down to a large pond in the park. It was sunset, and I remember just being so present with each other and so happy.

That is, until I felt a slap on my arm. Startled, I looked over at Stefanie, and she said, "Tag—you're it!" Then she sprinted off across the lawn.

I thought to myself, *This is what life is all about: sweet, fun times together.* Then I powered up my legs like Sonic the Hedgehog and took off after her. We let every care drop off of us as we played that afternoon. To this day, it is one of my favorite memories together.

Heavenly Father, help me to show my wife how important she is to me with the time I choose to spend with her. *Help us both to set aside time to be present with each other, giving one another our full attention. I pray that as we spend time together, our intimacy will grow stronger, and we will get to know each other better.*

Help my wife to make spending time with me a priority, and show her how to go out of her way to make me feel special. When we are together, help her to let her worries and fears go, and allow her to feel fully alive. Break off any pain from the past, and help us to heal any wounds that would keep us apart.

I pray that our marriage is full of laughter, joy, and peace as we choose to spend quality time together. Father, time is such a gift. Help my wife to take full advantage of the time we have, and help me to never take her for granted. Show us Your loving-kindness through our interactions with each other. In all we do, I pray we would grow closer to each other and to You. Amen.

Quality time is the fertilizer to the growth of your marriage relationship.

love in action . . .

Together: Spend some quality time together in a way that fills you both. Plan to make this part of your routine.

For her: Make time in your schedule for something you know your wife would love to do, and invite her to be a part of it.

WEEK

29

UNFAMILIAR TERRITORY

A prayer that she will develop her spiritual gifts

A spiritual gift is given to each of us so we can help each other.

1 CORINTHIANS 12:7

I was horrible at praying when we first got married. I was unsure what to pray, and often I had a very transactional relationship with God. *You scratch my back, and I'll scratch yours* was how I approached prayer. It wasn't until I met Stefanie that my prayer life began to change.

She would always ask me to pray. I was used to doing this before meals and when I was sobbing after a breakup, but praying for our car ride? This was unfamiliar territory, but it began to develop a muscle in my faith that had been unused for many years.

One thing I did not want to do was quench Stefanie's desire and need for prayer. It was important to her, she was gifted at it, and she needed it often. I always wondered why she didn't just pray herself instead of asking me, but I believe it was God's way of training me, humbling me, and showing His desire for a deeper connection. What better way to do that than through the woman I loved?

Giving your wife space to grow and allowing her to cultivate her gifting will change your marriage for the better. My prayer is that you will use your gifting to encourage your wife to become all God calls her to be.

Heavenly Father, show me how I can encourage my wife in her natural talents, but also in her spiritual gifting. *You have uniquely gifted my wife to serve You. Reveal to her the ways You want to use her to help others, and give her the capacity and courage to go for it. Help me to never quench her desire to follow You with her whole heart.*

I pray that as we both discover our giftings, we can use them to grow closer to You. Together we can do amazing things for Your Kingdom. I pray against the enemy who seeks to divide us and cause us to discourage each other. And I ask that You would help us to be open to whatever ways You want to use us to encourage others in the future. Amen.

Each person is given spiritual gifts to be able to bless and encourage others.

love in action . . .

Together: Take a spiritual giftings test. Discuss how you can support each other in using your gifts.

For her: Encourage your wife by calling out examples of how she has used her gifts well.

Father,
may our marriage
be full of laughter,
joy, and peace
as we choose
to spend time together.
Help us never take
each other for granted.

WEEK 30

A PLACE TO BELONG

A prayer for strong church community

They worshiped together at the Temple each day, met in homes for the Lord's Supper, and shared their meals with great joy and generosity—all the while praising God and enjoying the goodwill of all the people. And each day the Lord added to their fellowship those who were being saved.

ACTS 2:46-47

Finding a good church community is one of the most valuable things you can do for your marriage. In seasons when we have had a strong church community and support, it has made a huge difference for us.

We have tried our fair share of Bible studies. For us, a joint study works best with our schedule. (Plus, we just love being together!) We have learned that not every group will be a good fit and that you have to keep trying until you find one that will uplift you, grow with you, and support you.

We recently found a group at our local church that is not specifically for couples. The members are of vastly different ages, careers, and stages of life, but it has been one of the most encouraging, peaceful, and growth-filled groups we have ever been a part of. We love it.

Where we could have gone wrong was by not continuing to look for a community after one group wasn't a fit. Or, we could have felt like we had to be married to a group even though it wasn't right for us or didn't uplift or challenge us.

To find a good church community, you have to put in some effort. But once you find one, it can be such a blessing.

Heavenly Father, I know that we need positive and encouraging voices to speak life over our marriage. *Will You give us the courage to look for a good church community? Help my wife to find a great group of friends. Reveal relationships that would be a blessing to her, and help her to remove any that are harmful to her faith, her health, or our marriage.*

I thank You for the great people we have in our lives already, and I pray that You will give us the ability to put effort into those relationships, choosing to be a blessing in any way we can. Help us to make community a priority, and even if it doesn't work well at first, help us to have endurance to continue looking for a great group to invest our time into.

I know that when my wife is poured into, she feels more encouraged, full of life, and able to be a good wife. Help me to be a leader in cultivating church relationships that will bless our marriage. Show us ways that we need to grow in this area. Protect my wife from any potential hurt or reminders of past wounds, and allow us to move forward with hope for the future. Amen.

Finding good church community is like taking a dip into a cold, refreshing spring after a long, hot hike.

love in action . . .

Together: Talk about ways to strengthen the connection to your church community. If you don't have one, make it a priority to find one.

—•—

For her: Be encouraging to your wife when she pursues positive connections.

WEEK

31

JOINT VENTURES

A prayer that she feels supported in her interests

Don't look out only for your own interests, but take an interest in others, too.

PHILIPPIANS 2:4

I never was one to really enjoy hiking. The thought of climbing up a huge mountain, only to come back down, or worse, going down only to trudge back up, was less than enticing. But when I met Stefanie, she was all about hiking. She loved it!

When I asked what she would like to do, oftentimes it would begin with a hike. Now, in situations like this, you have three options: go with it, compromise, or completely shut it down. I didn't particularly want to hike *any* mountain, but there were plenty I definitely *didn't* want to climb. So I would mention a trail I wouldn't mind—a compromise.

Differing interests is one area where marriages can get off track. We don't enjoy the same activities our spouse does, so we each do our own thing. Sometimes this can be healthy. But it's powerful when we can take an interest in a pastime our spouse enjoys. It's a way to love them.

Since we've been together, we have hiked all over the world, seeing beautiful places I would never have visited without Stefanie. My life has been enriched because I chose to take on her interests. Now I love hiking with her. Take interest in what your wife loves. It's an easy way to love her each day and to strengthen the bond between you.

Heavenly Father, I thank You for the unique way You created my wife. *I appreciate the interests, passions, and talents You have given her. Help me to cultivate her desire for those interests each day. Show me ways that I can grow as a person through my involvement in her passions, and help us to grow closer as we do them together. I pray that I can support her in any way that helps her to grow as a person and brings life and love to our marriage.*

Reveal to her any involvement that has become an idol or stronghold in her life, and help her to remove it. I love seeing my wife happy, so show me ways to encourage her so she can live a joyful life. I pray that as we do more together, we can grow in intimacy, and that our love for each other will multiply. Help her to take an interest in the things that I love doing as well. Our marriage is blessed when we both feel filled spiritually, relationally, and physically, so help us pursue things that build us up. Thank You for giving me a partner to enjoy my favorite things with. Amen.

The more you invest in your wife's interests, the stronger your marriage will be.

love in action . . .

Together: Look for ways to include each other in your individual interests.

—•—

For her: Take time to do something with your wife that she enjoys. Show that what is important to her is important to you.

WEEK

32

OF RUBBER TIRES AND COOKIES

A prayer for health and well-being

Dear friend, I hope all is well with you and that you are as healthy in body as you are strong in spirit.

3 JOHN 1:2

I could probably eat a rubber tire and feel just fine afterward. It seems like my stomach can handle most anything.

Stefanie, on the other hand, has a ton of food allergies—gluten, soy, and corn to name a few. Finding foods that work can be a challenge. I've learned to shop at places like Trader Joe's and Whole Foods, making my way to the gluten-free section and seeking out items we can enjoy together.

One evening early in our marriage, I offered to make cookies for us. I was excited to try a new dough I had found. I made the cookies, and boy did they taste good for gluten-free. Stefanie thought the same.

But the next few days were rough. Stefanie's stomach hurt so badly, and we couldn't figure out why. Finally, I took a second look at the flour I had bought, only to realize that I had mistakenly grabbed one that was organic but not gluten-free. I felt terrible for what my confusion had put Stefanie through.

I now consider myself a seasoned veteran when it comes to allergies and intolerances. Like anything else, it requires being intentional, genuinely wanting to help your spouse, and choosing to learn new things. Now we can enjoy many great foods together—even cookies!

Heavenly Father, I lift up my wife's health to You. *I pray for her physical condition, that You would strengthen her and heal her from any sickness. I also lift up her mental health, that she would have a sound mind, relying on Your truth over her heart, and that You would keep her free from any unproductive or sinful thoughts. Please cover her emotional health as well, that she would not let her feelings get the best of her but have control over how she feels and be able to express herself in appropriate ways.*

Please keep me physically, emotionally, and mentally healthy as well. Help us both to do things daily, within our ability, that would benefit ourselves and each other. Convict us both of any ways that we are being unhealthy, and guide us toward better choices. Show us nutritious eating habits, manageable exercise options, and ways to positively contribute to each other's emotional and mental well-being. You are so good to us. I pray that we will have a long life together, full of happiness and joy. Amen.

Looking out for your wife's well-being yields benefits for her *and* for you.

love in action . . .

Together: Set goals to support each other in all aspects of your health—physical, mental, and emotional.

—•—

For her: Take time to care for your own health so you're able to be supportive of your wife.

WEEK

33

HELPING HANDS

A prayer for a servant's heart

Don't use your freedom to satisfy your sinful nature. Instead, use your freedom to serve one another in love.

GALATIANS 5:13

Stefanie has always had an incredible heart for serving others. Even during times that we have been struggling to make ends meet, she has looked for ways to be a blessing to others.

One day, during the 2020 pandemic, we got a call from our church in Los Angeles. They were looking for volunteers to help pass out food to the homeless. I was hesitant, but Stefanie jumped all over it. So after taking the proper precautions, we headed over.

Our church's homeless ministry fed thousands per month throughout the city. They had set up a drive-through area in the parking lot where people in need could pick up their food for the day at no cost.

When we pulled up to the church, Stefanie was out of the car quickly and ready to jump in line to help. Any apprehension I had vanished when I saw her kindly talking to people, praying for them, and handing out meals. Her servant's heart was evident, and it made me always want to cultivate that desire in her for helping others and to fan it into flame whenever I could. That servant's heart has rubbed off on me, too, and I have found that when you serve others in need, you often feel like the one who benefits the most.

Heavenly Father, I pray today for my wife's heart. *Your Word says that it is better to serve than to be served. Help us both to have a servant's heart, not only toward each other, but toward those in our community. Reveal to my wife anything that would cause her to be selfish or hold her back from serving others. Show her specific ways to use her gifts for those in need.*

I ask that You would reveal any areas in our marriage where she can serve me as her husband, and please help me to also find ways to serve her as my wife. I pray that through service we would be filled with Your love and grow closer to You in the process. Help me to surrender any pride in my heart and find ways to be a blessing to my wife each day. Help us both to make time to serve in our community and at our church whenever possible. I pray that humility and service would be two things we would cultivate in our marriage going forward. Amen.

It is a greater gift to serve than to be served.

love in action . . .

Together: Find a church project, outreach ministry, or community service that you can take part in.

—— • ——

For her: Watch for a task your wife normally does that you can do instead to love and serve her.

Father, I appreciate
the interests, passions,
and talents You have given
my wife. Help me support her
in any way that helps
her to grow.

WEEK

34

FOLLOWING GOD'S CALL

A prayer that she will embrace her purpose in Christ

God is working in you, giving you the desire and the power to do what pleases him.

PHILIPPIANS 2:13

Do you love seeing your wife thrive? When Stefanie is walking within her purpose, there is hardly anything more attractive to me. She is incredibly gifted in showing empathy, developing strategy, and helping people in their darkest moments.

God has taken us to a lot of places with our ministry. One time we visited a mall in Billings, Montana, where Stefanie was to speak about the value of each individual and who they were created to be. We were just starting our relationship courses and curriculum, so this was a good step toward sharing what God had put on her heart.

She was so nervous, but I encouraged her to be herself and allow God to speak through her. The mall was in full weekend-shopper mode, and Stefanie knocked it out of the park. Many people came up to her afterward to share how her stories had impacted them.

It is incredibly powerful to be there to encourage and support our wives. When God is the center, and when they feel our support, nothing can stand in the way. God has never let me down when I have set out to serve Stefanie in her purpose. If God has been stirring your wife's heart in some way, seek to understand her dreams and desires, and do what you can to unequivocally support her.

Heavenly Father, I appreciate all the qualities, talents, and abilities You have given my wife that make her so special. *I pray that You would open up any doors that would allow her to fully live out Your purpose. Additionally, I pray that You would close any doors that would keep her from pursuing that purpose. Give me the wisdom, strength, and humility to serve her in whatever way would help her achieve her goals.*

I pray against the enemy in any way that he is trying to keep her from fully being who You called her to be. I ask that You would be the firm foundation for her to stand on no matter what she faces. Show her the path to take, and give her clear direction and the capacity to fully carry out the call You have placed on her life. Help me to always love and support her to the best of my ability so that she will run to You and fully commit to Your plans for her. Amen.

A purpose-driven life is one filled with hope, peace, and fulfillment.

love in action . . .

Together: Find ways to take steps toward your purpose as a couple. Discover what God has called you to, and obediently walk it out.

—— • ——

For her: Find out what your wife's passion or dream is. Ask God for wisdom in helping her pursue His purpose for her.

WEEK

35

LIFELINE TO FREEDOM

A prayer for breaking strongholds

We use God's mighty weapons, not worldly weapons, to knock down the strongholds of human reasoning and to destroy false arguments.

2 CORINTHIANS 10:4

I've mentioned before that throughout my early years, I had one dream: to become a professional athlete. I dedicated myself wholeheartedly to this ambition, and eventually, I earned a college basketball scholarship. But then came that career-ending injury that left me shattered and struggling to make sense of it all.

I had always maintained a deep connection with God, striving to live a life of faith and righteousness. Yet when my dream crumbled, my confidence, hope, and sense of purpose plummeted into despair.

Desperate to find worth anew, I turned to various pursuits. One became a powerful stronghold: video games. I immersed myself in a virtual world, seeking solace and escape. Nights turned into days, weekends slipped away, and I even missed classes as I delved into a realm where I could be anyone I wished.

Breaking free from this addiction took several grueling years. I had conquered it once before I met Stefanie, but during a challenging period I reverted to old habits.

Thankfully, by the grace of God, Stefanie walked alongside me in those dark moments. Her unwavering prayers became my lifeline, and I learned a powerful lesson: the only stronghold we should ever embrace is the one God builds around us for our protection, peace, and love. Any other stronghold should be willingly surrendered to the Lord.

Heavenly Father, strongholds in our hearts and minds can lead us to prideful postures and defensive attitudes. *I pray today that You would break any strongholds in my wife's heart, in the name of Jesus. Help her release any worries, pains, or fears that are causing her to shut herself off from You, me, or others. My wife can thrive when she feels free from these concerns. Help her to prioritize time with You so that she can know your peace.*

I pray against any hurtful experiences from the past or any lies spoken against her that would cause my wife to block her heart. Help her with any unhealthy, addictive behavior, and allow her to submit it before You. If there is anything in her heart or mind that would work against our marriage, I pray that You would remove it and replace it with Your truth. Please help us be united in our decisions, our conversations, and our daily activities. Help my wife to live to her fullest potential today and every day. Amen.

The only stronghold you are meant to have is the one built around you by God, full of hope, promise, peace, and love.

love in action . . .

Together: Talk about any major lies, habits, or mindsets that might be holding you back in your marriage. Make a plan to seek peace from these strongholds.

For her: Take inventory of your life, and commit to dealing with any strongholds that may be interfering with your relationship with your wife.

WEEK

36

COMBATING DOUBT

A prayer for overcoming doubt

I am convinced that nothing can ever separate us from God's love. Neither death nor life, neither angels nor demons, neither our fears for today nor our worries about tomorrow—not even the powers of hell can separate us from God's love.

ROMANS 8:38

The hardest thing we have been through in our marriage is the loss of our twin baby boys, Asher and Shiloh. We had been trying for many years to get pregnant without success, until one year, on my birthday, we learned we were going to be parents. I had never seen Stefanie so happy.

At our first ultrasound, we were filled with joy to learn that we were having twins. That is, until the nurse told us there were no heartbeats. In just one moment, we went from the highest high to the lowest low. We left in tears, questioning why this could happen.

Our home had never felt emptier. In complete despair, Stefanie asked me what we should do. All I could think of was to worship God. Overwhelmed with doubt, fear, and disappointment, we chose to sing praise to the Father, believing that no matter what, He is good.

What followed was the hardest season of our lives, but we placed a stake in the ground that day and determined that in this difficult place, we would serve God because He is worthy. Stefanie has often told me about the impact of that day on her, and when we face future seasons of doubt, we know how to respond.

Heavenly Father, I am so grateful for the wife You have blessed me with. *Help me to always take time to build her up and encourage her through life's challenges. Encourage her today with Your words of truth, and give her strength to accomplish the tasks before her. When doubt crosses her mind, I ask that You would provide peace, clarity, and wisdom. When she questions herself, doubts her decisions, or second-guesses her choices, I pray that You would give her assurance as she trusts in You. Provide her with the grace to make the right choices, and when she messes up, help her to learn and grow rather than getting discouraged.*

Father, help me to encourage her about what she has done well and to foster in her the confidence to continue pushing forward in growth. I pray that when we doubt, we would still choose to worship You because You are worthy and You are always good. Help us encourage one another when we have doubts. I pray against anything that is not of You in our marriage. Help us to entrust all of our decisions and actions to Your loving hands. Amen.

Encouragement and worship can break the seeds of doubt.

love in action . . .

Together: Offer thanksgiving and praise for the good things God has done; watch the doubts and fears become smaller as God becomes bigger and bigger.

For her: When your wife has doubts, be quick to offer encouragement and prayer.

WEEK

37

FLIPPING THE SCRIPT

A prayer for a positive attitude

Throw off your old sinful nature and your former way of life. . . . Instead, let the Spirit renew your thoughts and attitudes. Put on your new nature, created to be like God—truly righteous and holy.

EPHESIANS 4:22-24

As sports fans, my wife and I have weathered many seasons of triumphs and disappointments. She hails from a family of die-hard Steelers fans, and since we've moved to Pittsburgh, where game day is a cherished tradition, I must admit, I've come to love watching the games together too. Now, I'm still a loyal Cowboys supporter, and that has led to some lively exchanges as we've navigated past rivalries and cheered each other's teams on.

To a Steelers fan, anything less than a Super Bowl victory feels like a season gone bad, but the team has faced its share of challenges. During one rough patch, we were gathered in my in-laws' basement for a game, and the air was thick with negativity.

But then, something remarkable happened. Stefanie began to say genuinely kind things about the players, the coaches, and the game. She flipped the script of our collective mood, even though it didn't change the outcome of the game. We had a choice: we could allow the final score to ruin our day, or we could simply enjoy being together.

The same principle applies to marriage. We can focus on the negative, or we can consciously shift our perspective and appreciate our blessings. I'm profoundly grateful to Stefanie for demonstrating this to me. Her example has not only improved my sports-watching experience but has also made me a better husband.

Heavenly Father, I lift up my wife's spirit and attitude to you. *Help her to be encouraged by the blessings around her. Let her heart reflect the love of Christ in everything that she does. I know that we are both more content when we know the other person is happy, so please let us show our positivity not only with our actions but with our words as well.*

Any major change must start in our hearts, and if I desire a change, I must be a leader in this area. So help me to be more positive in my thinking. Show me the blessings around me so that I can be grateful each moment. Let that gratitude overflow into positivity in our lives. My wife works so hard for our family. Help me to reciprocate her actions, and help us to grow closer because of the positive atmosphere we build in our marriage. Amen.

Positivity is an attitude. Choose to fix your eyes on the blessings in your life each day.

love in action . . .

Together: Select a container to use for collecting notes about blessings in your life. Periodically review these notes of gratitude together.

For her: Begin filling a container with encouraging notes for your wife. In difficult times, present her with the container.

WEEK

38

JUST TURN IT OFF

A prayer for guarding her thoughts

Fix your thoughts on what is true, and honorable, and right, and pure, and lovely, and admirable. Think about things that are excellent and worthy of praise.

PHILIPPIANS 4:8

Stefanie and I love to watch shows together. It's one way that we connect over similar interests. Often, we will pause the show to talk about what is going on and try to predict what will happen next.

Because we want to protect ourselves from any thoughts, feelings, or views that would take away from our marriage, we are very careful about what we consume. Our rule is that we won't watch anything above a TV-14 rating (or PG-13 for movies). Even when a show is within that rating limit, if we sense it is pushing the limits of our integrity, we will agree to turn it off. No matter how good the show is.

One year, we got caught up in the show *Suits*. We really enjoyed the plot and the actors, but we started to notice that after watching it, we became more contentious with each other. I finally told Stefanie that I thought we should stop watching it. She chose to trust me, and we stopped right then and there. We had enjoyed that show, but it was not worth the fighting it provoked between us.

Since then, we have applied the same rule to anything that is not from God and that threatens our unity. Protecting our thoughts, hearts, and attitudes in this way has been such a blessing in our marriage.

Heavenly Father, I pray today that You would protect my wife's mind from any thoughts, feelings, or motives that are not from You and that would lead her away from You or our marriage. *It's easy to let our thoughts or feelings dwell on negative things such as jealousy, comparison, or greed. I ask that You would protect her mind from the lies of the enemy and that You would instead fill her thoughts with the fruit of the Spirit.*

Help us both to be mindful and careful of the things we consume, whether on social media, in the shows we watch, or at events we attend. Keep us from any love of sin, and help us to always fix our eyes on You. I know that our marriage is blessed when we take time to enjoy each other and choose to see the blessings around us. Help us to think about the things of heaven and not the things of this earth. Teach me ways to be a leader in this area and fight, even when it's uncomfortable, for my wife's peace of mind and heart. Amen.

What you watch matters. Choose to protect your thoughts, heart, and attitude from things that aren't from God.

love in action . . .

Together: Talk about the shows you consume as a couple. Set ground rules that will be life-bringing for your marriage.

—•—

For her: If anything you watch is taking you outside of your integrity, choose to seek content that will be uplifting and encouraging in your marriage.

WEEK

39

EVERYONE HAS A STORY

A prayer for a heart of compassion

When he saw the crowds, he had compassion on them because they were confused and helpless, like sheep without a shepherd.

MATTHEW 9:36

Stefanie has always had a heart for others. She has gone on missions trips to New Orleans and Rwanda to help those in need. I have always admired her ability to put herself in other people's shoes and see things the way they might see them. It makes her an incredible partner as we look to help other people in our business.

When we lived in Los Angeles, we would see homeless people on almost every corner asking for money or food. It's incredibly disheartening. In the past, I lacked compassion for people like this, assuming they could get their life back together if they wanted to.

Seeing Stefanie be kind to each and every person on the street changed my heart for the homeless. She would buy them food, pray over their ailments, and look them in the eyes. She would remind me that they have a story, probably one with immense pain that led to their current situation.

Seeing her compassion shifted my perspective and allowed me to see them as people created by God. In the same way, we can encourage our wives to act from a heart of love instead of judgment, and together we can bring hope and help to the hurting.

Heavenly Father, I pray today that You would give my wife a heart of compassion for those around her. *Allow her the capacity to see other people from Your perspective and through Your lens of love. Inspire her to be kind to others and empathetic to their needs. Give her opportunities to share hope with those who are hurting.*

Help me to fan the flame of compassion in our marriage. Show us ways that we can be a support to others. Inspire us to be considerate of their needs and to take action to supply those needs. Reveal any areas in our hearts that are keeping us from being compassionate. When we serve and love others, our capacity for compassion grows. Father, You are love, and love comes from You. I pray that we grow in our passion to serve You with all of our hearts and to fully trust You in every area. Help us both to grow in kindness and generosity. Amen.

Compassion helps us realize the needs of others and how we can love them like Christ.

love in action . . .

Together: Look for ways to serve others in need so that compassion becomes a cornerstone of your marriage.

—•—

For her: Think of ways you can be a model to your wife of compassion and empathy for others.

Father,
protect my wife
from thoughts and feelings
that are not from You.
Help her to always
fix her eyes on You.

WEEK

40

THE COMPARISON TRAP

A prayer that she will find her identity in God

You are a chosen people. You are royal priests, a holy nation, God's very own possession. As a result, you can show others the goodness of God, for he called you out of the darkness into his wonderful light.

1 PETER 2:9

Being on social media comes with its own set of blessings and hardships. We are blessed to help so many people around the world, and it has brought us many other opportunities.

But one of the hard parts is the inevitable negative comments. Like anyone else in the public eye, we've seen some pretty nasty things written about us, our ministry, and our marriage. Another challenge is comparison. This can be a struggle with such a constant view of other people's successes.

When we face these negatives, we have learned to shift our mindset to the truth. Each day when we wake up, we spend time reading God's Word before we ever open our phones. This discipline wasn't easy at first, but it has become a part of our routine.

When you open your phone, you are bombarded with messages about your value. If that is the first input you receive each day, it is easy to start believing it. But when you start with the source of love and truth, those other messages come off as counterfeit. You are able to claim the truth much more easily. Whether social media is part of your work or just a pastime, taking this approach can help you and your wife remember your value in God's eyes.

Heavenly Father, I pray that my wife would receive the amazing truths of Your Word about her value. *Help her to run to You when she gets discouraged. I pray that Your words of love will pour over her like a refreshing waterfall. Speak directly to any insecurities, fears, or lies about who she is, her identity in You, and her status as my wife. Grow her knowledge of Scripture so that when hurtful situations come up, she can rely on Your truth.*

I pray that I will be a leader in the home so that I can always point her back to You. Help me take time each day to speak life, hope, and love over my wife. Give me wisdom to know when she needs encouragement, and speak through me to her heart. I pray that we always rely on You as our foundation when times get tough and that we would always choose truth over any lie of the enemy. Block out any voices of negativity and bind the enemy in Jesus' mighty name. You are our good Father, and we trust You with our marriage. Amen.

> **The first thing you put into your mind each day matters. Seek to receive God's truth before anything else.**

love in action . . .

Together: Go through a Bible study or devotional to receive God's truth and encouragement.

—— • ——

For her: When your wife gets discouraged by negative words or comparisons, remind her of where her true value and identity lie.

A PASSION FOR LEARNING

A prayer for growth and transformation

The Lord—who is the Spirit—makes us more and more like him as we are changed into his glorious image.

2 CORINTHIANS 3:18

I love Stefanie's passion and fervor for growth. She always wants to learn and improve so that we can have the best possible life together.

I have benefited greatly from this in many areas. Thankfully, God has worked out a lot of the pride in me so I can be open to new ways of thinking and willing to consider areas in which I might need to grow or in which I have gotten complacent. After my college basketball career ended, I no longer had physical goals to work toward. Quite frankly, I stopped really taking care of myself, which led to weight gain and depression.

Stefanie would tell me about the benefits of healthy eating and daily exercise. We walked and hiked, and I began to eat more of these green things called vegetables. With better habits and my willingness to try new things, the pounds seemed to fall right off.

One of the greatest gifts you can give your marriage is a willingness to listen and to grow. There is so much more for you as you challenge each other and progress together. As you cultivate an environment of growth, you will both bring ideas to the table that benefit your marriage.

Heavenly Father, I pray today that You would inspire my wife to always continue growing. *Help identify areas in which she can develop, so that she can continue to go after the calling You have placed on her. Reveal any areas in which she has resisted growth, and encourage her to step out and move forward. Break any strongholds that would keep her stuck or stagnant, and develop a spiritual fervor for Your words of truth and hope.*

Show me ways that I can motivate her toward growth through my words, actions, finances, or encouragement. Unite us in this vision, and reveal any ways that we can grow together. Help me never to be complacent with my own life, but spur me on to be the best version of myself and the best possible husband to her. Allow us to grow in love, hope, and purpose for all the days of our lives as we pursue You. Amen.

When you have an open mind, you can grow in ways you never thought possible.

love in action . . .

Together: Set some small, achievable goals for three ways you want to grow as a couple.

—— • ——

For her: Thank your wife for the ways she has helped you grow and has made you a better person.

WEEK

42

JUST FOR FUN

A prayer for lightheartedness

A cheerful heart is good medicine,
but a broken spirit saps a person's strength.

PROVERBS 17:22

One of my favorite things in the whole world is when Stefanie gives me a smile or laughs with me. One thing that makes her smile is a visit to Disneyland.

We have always loved going there together. We act like little children all day, excited to be in a fantasy world. We run around trying to find Mickey Mouse, yelling, "ARRR!" at the Pirates of the Caribbean, and dancing to the music of the Main Street parade.

Those moments of joy bring warmth to my heart. For a few hours, we don't have to think about our mortgage, putting food on the table, or what the future might bring. It's about living wholeheartedly and lightheartedly, fully in the moment.

We have made it a priority to invest in experiences like these in our marriage. We ask for Disneyland tickets for our birthdays, and we head to downtown Pittsburgh for the holidays to see all of the Santas and dance to the Christmas music. Joy is the secret for a happy, healthy marriage. It's not that we're pretending our cares and concerns aren't there. It's just our way of choosing not to let them get the best of us. We've both faced so much that could have broken us. That's why we try to choose joy each day in even the briefest moments together.

Heavenly Father, I pray for a spirit of joy and lightheartedness to abound in our marriage. *There are so many things that can tear us down or make us sad. I pray that we can choose joy in every circumstance. Help us to find ways to be more carefree. We know that worrying never helps, so I pray that we will choose to be more lighthearted in our everyday interactions and conversations. I pray that my wife will choose to smile more than she frowns. I pray for the sounds of laughter to fill all the corners of our house.*

Father, I know my wife will feel more fulfilled when her heart is full of joy. Help me to bring a smile to her with thoughtful actions, kind words, and silly gestures throughout the day. Encourage my wife in the areas she needs it the most, and help us to fully enjoy each and every moment for the gift that it is. I am so thankful for this life You have given to us. I pray we would cherish all of our blessings. Amen.

Joy is the secret to a happy, healthy marriage.

love in action . . .

Together: Plan an activity just for fun. Choose to be spontaneous and laugh together more.

—— • ——

For her: Do something silly that will make your wife laugh.

IT ONLY TAKES A MOMENT

A prayer that she feels recognized and appreciated

Love each other with genuine affection, and take delight in honoring each other.
ROMANS 12:10

Stefanie and I have demanding jobs that require us to be "on" for most of the day—working with our clients, doing podcast interviews, and putting out content to encourage people. We often feel drained when we're finished, and many times it feels like a thankless job.

One thing Stefanie does to help rejuvenate my spirit is slipping a little note under my journal every morning while I am reading my Bible. Often it says how much she loves me or how much she enjoyed a particular adventure.

But I love most of all when she tells me how much she appreciates all that I do for our family and that she is happy and content in our marriage.

When I hear those words, the weight drops off my shoulders and I feel like all the hard work is worth it. Those notes take only a moment of her time, but they make a massive difference in my day, my mindset, and my attitude going forward.

My dad used to say, "It only takes a moment to be courteous." I find that in marriage this is especially true—and courtesy includes showing appreciation. That single moment can make the biggest difference in your spouse's day. I know it always has for me.

Heavenly Father, I pray that today and every day my wife would feel acknowledged and appreciated for all she does for our family. *Show me ways that I can encourage her through my words and actions for what she contributes to our life. I pray for moments of pause and celebration when she can feel recognized for who she is. Help me to never take who she is or what she does for granted.*

Reveal ways that we can appreciate each other more in our everyday lives, and help us to go to You as our source of life even when we don't get encouragement from each other. The enemy wants us to resent each other and seeks to divide us. I pray against the enemy in Jesus' name. I pray that gratitude and thankfulness would be cornerstones of our communication and attitude with each other. Help my wife know how much I love her and how loved she is by You every moment of the day. Amen.

It only takes a moment to show appreciation and recognition.

love in action . . .

Together: Spend an evening celebrating each other for the things you appreciate, including the sacrifices and the kindness.

—•—

For her: Leave a small note of appreciation in a place your wife will discover it during her day.

WEEK
44

ACTIVE LISTENING

A prayer that she feels heard

A truly wise person uses few words; a person with understanding is even-tempered.

PROVERBS 17:27

"How do you feel about how I feel?" Stefanie asked, in the midst of what was turning into an argument.

Her question pulled me up short. I had never been challenged to view a discussion this way before. She had been telling me about a problem at work, and I had immediately tried to fix it for her and explain away the other parties' actions.

This was the source of many arguments early in our marriage. Stefanie would bring up something to me, and I would get defensive, try to fix it, and then tell her how what she was feeling was wrong.

It wasn't until she asked me that question—how I felt about how she was feeling—that I began to understand. All she really wanted was for me to listen, understand her feelings, and be empathetic. Active listening involves repeating back what she says, so she knows I am tracking with her. This shows I am truly present in the conversation.

I am nowhere near perfect at this, and I still tend to downplay her feelings and encourage her to think positively. But when I can fully give her my attention, listen, and relate to her issues, she feels heard. She feels supported by me as her husband, and we can move on.

Heavenly Father, I pray for clarity in our communication. *Help us to be kind with our words and direct with what we are trying to say. I pray that my wife will always feel heard and understood. Help me to give her my full attention and be present with her. Enable me to identify and repeat back gently the things that are important to her and that she wants me to remember. Give me patience when she is upset, and give me wisdom to hold back on positive words or solutions until she is ready for them.*

Give me empathy for how she feels, and help me to express that to her when we talk with each other. Help me to hold my tongue when I don't have something helpful to say, and let my words build her up rather than tear her down.

Allow Your truth to ring loud in all our conversations, and help us to speak out of that truth rather than from pain. Grow our communication daily so that we can help each other in the best ways possible. Amen.

Active listening lets her know you care, you are present, and you can relate to how she is feeling.

love in action . . .

Together: Practice active listening—letting each other talk fully about a concern without immediately jumping in to fix it.

For her: When your wife brings up an issue, ask questions and repeat back what you hear so she knows you understand.

WEEK

45

RELIABILITY

A prayer for relationships built on trust

Just say a simple, "Yes, I will," or "No, I won't." Anything beyond this is from the evil one.

MATTHEW 5:37

Stefanie is hands down one of the most dependable people I've ever known. What sets her apart is her unwavering commitment to reliability. She takes this very seriously, managing her commitments with precision on her trusty calendar.

I'm not quite as well organized when it comes to calendars. Don't get me wrong—most of the time, I've got everything under control, but I've occasionally missed important events simply because I forgot to jot them down. Needless to say, this has led to a few bumps in our marriage, when I've unintentionally let Stefanie down.

The worst part is the disappointment in *myself* when I see that I've disappointed *her*. I know how important it is to be reliable, not only to Stefanie but to myself and others as well. I've been on a journey to get better organized, diligently noting tasks and checking and rechecking schedules to make sure nothing slips through the cracks.

Reliability, I've learned, requires conscious effort. I'm incredibly fortunate to have Stefanie by my side. She's been patient and understanding, offering gentle reminders and guidance when needed. She's my rock, constantly helping me grow as a person and become a better friend to others.

Heavenly Father, I lift up my wife in the area of reliability. *I pray that her yes would be yes and that she would follow through on any commitment she makes. Give her strong boundaries so that she can enjoy the activities she wants and still make good on commitments she has made to me and others. I pray that she will have self-control and that she will not obsess about circumstances outside of her control.*

Help me to be a stable and reliable partner to her as well. Our relationship works best when we can trust each other. Give me wisdom to know when to say yes to obligations and when to say no, and help my wife always to be able to depend on me. Give me strength to follow through on her requests of me, and give her understanding when I fall short.

I pray for open, honest, and clear communication in our marriage. I pray that we can rely on Your strength, knowing that You will never let us down. Help us both to have a servant's heart in our dealings with each other and with other people. Help us to wholeheartedly trust You with everything. Amen.

Being a reliable person builds trust in your relationships.

love in action . . .

Together: Talk about your strengths and weaknesses in reliability. Game-plan how you can both be more trustworthy going forward.

—•—

For her: Apologize for any ways you have let your wife down recently. Do what you can to rebuild trust going forward.

Father, I pray
that my wife would feel
appreciated for all she does.
May gratitude be a cornerstone
of our communication.

A FOREIGN CONCEPT?

A prayer for good self-care habits

He lets me rest in green meadows; he leads me beside peaceful streams. He renews my strength. He guides me along right paths, bringing honor to his name.

PSALM 23:2-3

When I first heard about self-care, it was a foreign concept to me. I grew up with the model of my parents' generation, who worked hard for everything they had and gave little thought to taking care of themselves. But I have learned that time for self-care is so important.

Often, Stefanie and I simultaneously work on several projects that take up enormous amounts of our time. It often means working weekends and long nights to get everything done. With that can come some consequences, such as neglecting to take care of ourselves.

To counteract this, we have taken a few steps to ensure we have time for breaks when we need them. I can let Stefanie know if I need an hour to enjoy a hobby, play video games, or go exercise. The same goes for her. She might watch a favorite reality show or give herself a facial.

When we make time to care for ourselves, we feel healthier and become more productive, more present with each other, and better at our jobs. It's funny how time away from work can help you accomplish more when you get back. I am thankful I have learned to incorporate self-care into our marriage and daily routine.

Heavenly Father, give my wife the time she needs to take care of herself. *I know that when she is able to tend to her needs, desires, and wants, she is equipped to do her work well and be a better wife. I appreciate all that she does to take care of others, so please give her the ability and desire to take care of herself as well. Reveal to her any areas in which she is neglecting her needs.*

I pray that she will let me know when she needs extra support so I can help her in any way that I can. Help us to strategize together to make room in our schedules for downtime. Allow me as her husband to take care of myself as well. Show me ways that I need to rejuvenate my own heart, mind, and life so that I can be the best husband I can be. You are our good Father. Please take care of my wife each day. Amen.

When you take time for self-care, you become healthier, more productive, and more present.

love in action . . .

Together: Discuss the activities that fill each other up. Find ways to incorporate them into your routine.

—•—

For her: Take at least half an hour to do something that fills your tank, so you are at your best as a husband.

WEEK

47

WISH COME TRUE

A prayer for her dreams and aspirations

Take delight in the Lord, *and he will give you your heart's desires.*

PSALM 37:4

Stefanie has always had a passion for animals. Growing up, she would chase down rabbits and bring them home as pets. To this day, she is fearless about interacting with animals.

Her favorites are dolphins, and one of her childhood dreams was to be a trainer. She thought it would be amazing to swim with dolphins.

When I was still working at the Christian school in California, teachers could get free passes to SeaWorld. One year I had to attend a conference in San Diego, so I planned for the two of us to visit the park while there. I could see the excitement on Stefanie's face. She loved the little tide pools where she could touch the starfish and other animals.

But what she didn't know was that I had also reserved a Dolphin Swim experience for her. When I told her, she almost cried. She was so excited she was dancing around. At the allotted time, she put on a wet suit and headed for the tank, and an ear-to-ear smile adorned her face the entire session.

Seeing Stefanie living fully and freely in one of her biggest dreams was incredible. I honestly think it brought me more joy than it brought her. Whether your wife's dreams involve a long-awaited adventure or a significant career goal, helping her to achieve one of those dreams is a remarkable gift—for her and for your relationship.

Heavenly Father, encourage my wife in the dreams You have placed on her heart. *I pray that she would feel comfortable to share those dreams with You and with me. Guide her to ways she can take steps toward those dreams. Show me how I can encourage her to step out boldly in pursuit of her passions and fulfill Your purpose in her life.*

Reveal ways that our dreams align, and help us to be unified in pursuing them together. Make our communication clear so we can plan for our future. Restore any brokenness in my wife's heart from letdowns or past wounds, and allow her to live fully today and each day going forward.

I pray for us both to have dreams for our marriage and our future together. No matter what, help us to fix our eyes on You and trust You with our dreams. Give us the eyes to see and ears to hear any specific plans You have for us, and make our hearts tender to sense Your closeness. Help my wife to achieve every dream on her heart that aligns with Your will. Amen.

Helping your wife achieve her dreams is one of the greatest gifts you can give *and* receive.

love in action . . .

Together: Start a dream journal with goals you want to accomplish as a couple, then take steps toward those dreams.

—•—

For her: Take steps to make one of your wife's dreams happen for her.

WEEK

48

UNDIVIDED ATTENTION

A prayer for good work-life boundaries

Be careful how you live. Don't live like fools, but like those who are wise. Make the most of every opportunity in these evil days.

EPHESIANS 5:15-16

Work can become all-consuming at times. It can be hard to turn off our brain from our job because there are always more individuals to reach, more people to impact, and more lives to be changed.

Stefanie and I found that we needed strong boundaries so we could be at peace and give each other our undivided time when we were done for the day. Since a lot of our work is on our phones, it was hard at first to put them away. But the stress was getting to us, causing contention and loss of sleep. It was time to implement some strategies to achieve a better balance.

First, we stopped looking at our phones as soon as we woke up in the morning. We don't open them before taking time to read our Bibles and pray. Second, we started keeping our phones on the opposite side of the house so we aren't tempted to look at them. Finally, we stopped having them with us on the couch when we are spending time together, so we are not distracted.

This has had a profound impact on us. We are more successful in our work, and we are more available to each other, which has led to more moments of fun and far less conflict. Setting boundaries doesn't take away your freedom; it actually sets you free.

Heavenly Father, I thank You for the ways that You have uniquely gifted my wife in her work and in her passions. *It is important to me that she sets healthy boundaries with her work. Give her the capacity to complete what she needs to in her workday and to be able to leave work in its rightful place. Help our home not to be only a place of work and striving, but rather a place of refuge and peace for both of us. Show me ways that I can help her mentally let go of work so she can be present with me in our time together.*

In the same way, help me to leave my work behind me when I come home or when we are spending time together. If I need to deal with a pressing task or I need her input, help me to communicate clearly my needs and desires, and allow us to handle the issue in a healthy way. I pray that we can be fully present with each other and enjoy the moments we share. I pray that our worth is never in our work but that it would come fully from You and who You created us to be. Amen.

Setting boundaries doesn't take away your freedom. It actually sets you free.

love in action . . .

Together: Set boundaries regarding work, and find ways to be more intentional with your time together.

—•—

For her: Think of ways you can put work aside and be more present with your wife.

WEEK

49

THE BRUSH-OFF

A prayer for feeling her voice matters

When she speaks, her words are wise,
and she gives instructions with kindness.
PROVERBS 31:26

"I think we're supposed to be on John 17 today," Stefanie said one morning as we were getting ready to read our Bibles.

I had quoted something to her from that chapter the night before, so I was confident that we had already read it. I dismissed her comment, saying, "No, we're on John 18 today."

She asked if I was sure and if I would be willing to check.

Whether out loud or only in my head, I huffed at her request. There was no way I could have missed a day.

But sure enough, as I looked back in my journal, I saw that I had skipped John 16. This hit me hard because I had been so quick to dismiss her voice. It got me thinking about how many other times I had simply ignored her before it turned out that I was wrong. That morning, I apologized and she accepted, and it was a good reminder to me that her voice matters.

It's easy to get so caught up in our own world that we miss the little moments that we could build trust and confidence. When we leave pride at the door, make space for our wives to share their opinion, and listen before we speak, we build trust and mutual respect in our communication.

Heavenly Father, I thank You for my wife. *I love hearing her opinions, her thoughts, and her feelings on a variety of issues. Her voice matters to me. I pray that You would give her the confidence to speak her mind with me and be comfortable sharing how she feels. Help her to feel heard when she speaks, and give me the wisdom and patience to listen before I speak.*

I know that in marriage the two become one and her voice matters just as much as mine. Show me ways that I might be shutting her down with my voice, and give her grace in handling me when I am overpowering. I pray that I can be gentle in listening to her. Help me to actively listen and show that I am engaged in what she has to say.

Please give her the grace to speak with gentleness and respect as well. When she speaks to me in a gentle and kind way, I can more easily receive what she has to say. Help our skills in communication to grow, and please heal any past wounds in this area. Amen.

Be quick to listen, slow to judge, and slow to dismiss her voice.

love in action . . .

Together: Determine ways to ensure that each of you has a chance to speak and that you make decisions together.

—•—

For her: At the next opportunity, make a point of asking your wife's opinion on a matter.

A GIVING HEART

A prayer for generosity

I have been a constant example of how you can help those in need by working hard. You should remember the words of the Lord Jesus: "It is more blessed to give than to receive."

ACTS 20:35

Through our work and missions trips, we have made friends all around the world. Stefanie has kept up with a few people she served on a trip to Rwanda after college. The people there seem so full of life and joy even though they don't have much. Stefanie has always wanted to continue to be generous to those she has developed relationships with.

One time we sent a camera to an orphanage in Rwanda so they could take pictures to be used in spreading the word about what they do, which would enable them to help more children.

Later, a Rwandan friend wanted to send her daughter to a good school but couldn't afford it. We didn't have a ton of extra money ourselves at the time, and to be honest, I was nervous about wiring money to Africa. I approached Stefanie with a plan that I would be comfortable with. She went to work and found a way to do it, and we were able to send enough money for the school year.

The mother soon sent pictures of her daughter in her school uniform, and the smile on her face made it worth every penny. Stefanie is such a generous person, always fighting for people everyone else seems to forget. And truly, my life has been blessed in abundance by seeing how generosity can change lives, even across the world.

Heavenly Father, I pray for generosity to abound in our marriage. *Help my wife to be openhearted in how she views finances and relationships, as well as in her career and passions. Encourage her through all the blessings that You have given us. Reveal any ways that she might be withholding from others or acting selfishly, and allow her to break free of that mindset.*

We know that those who give will receive far more from You, Father. So please give us opportunities as a couple to be generous to each other and to those around us. Provide enough in our finances so that we can be generous to those in need. Show us ways to get involved in our community as givers, and help us to be obedient when You call us to generosity. Thank You, Father, for all Your good gifts to us, including each other. Help us to make generosity a staple in our lives. Amen.

It is far better to give than to receive.

love in action . . .

Together: Think of ways you can be generous to someone in need, such as sponsoring a child, donating time or money to your church, or serving your community.

—— • ——

For her: Watch for small ways you can be generous to your wife without expecting anything in return.

WEEK

51

HURTFUL WORDS

A prayer for healing from friendship wounds

Most important of all, continue to show deep love for each other, for love covers a multitude of sins.

1 PETER 4:8

The deepest moment of pain in our marriage was also, sadly, the moment we experienced our deepest friendship wound.

Fresh in the pain of our miscarriage, we were reeling. My heart broke for Stefanie as she lay on the couch with empty arms that should have been filled with her babies.

So many people reached out in support and kindness. We received unexpected packages from people we hadn't talked to in years but whose hearts felt our pain. We so appreciated their thoughtfulness.

But one of our closest friends seemed to be growing distant. The silence was strange, but Stefanie reached out because she needed the encouragement of a friend. The conversation that ensued pierced our hearts like a dagger. How could someone who had meant so much to us be so hurtful in our most difficult moment?

It was one more blow to our hearts, and I spent time listening to and hugging Stefanie through the loss of a friend on top of the loss of our twins. It was devastating, yet God never wastes anything. Friendship breakups can be hard to walk through, but I learned so much in that season about being a support, listening more than speaking, and providing shelter in the midst of life's storms.

Heavenly Father, I pray today over any friendship pain my wife may experience. *Friendships can be the source of so much joy, but they can also cause the deepest wounds. Protect my wife's heart from anyone who would seek to hurt her or who would cause her pain through their actions. Give her wisdom about how to navigate the ups and downs of relationships. Help me to support her and encourage her when friendships seem to be causing more pain than joy. Allow us to build connections together with other couples who would be an encouragement. Mend any past wounds, and guide us to community that would be healing and peaceful. Show us areas that we can grow in friendship with others, and help us to be quick to apologize or reconcile when we hurt them. You have brought so many good people into our lives. Allow us to be good friends to them. I love You, Father. Amen.*

Friendships can be a great source of joy, but they can also cause some of our deepest pain.

love in action . . .

Together: Talk about how you can be better friends to others and whether you need to seek healing in any current friendships.

For her: Seek to support your wife in her friendships that are life-bringing. If she is experiencing friendship hurt, give her a safe space to talk.

WEEK

52

TRAVEL MODE

A prayer for meaningful time away together

Come, my love, let us go out to the fields and spend the night among the wildflowers. Let us get up early and go to the vineyards to see if the grapevines have budded, if the blossoms have opened, and if the pomegranates have bloomed. There I will give you my love.

SONG OF SONGS 7:11-12

Stefanie and I love to get away together for adventures, traveling the world and meeting new people. Early in our marriage, we prioritized investing in such memories. Even on work trips we plan time for something fun.

Our favorite trip was to Punta Mita, Mexico. We had been hired by a hotel there to explore their property, try their food, and then share our experience on social media. In return, we got an eight-day, all-expenses-paid stay.

In the first couple of days, we knocked out everything we needed to do for work—pictures, writing, videos—so we could relax and enjoy the rest of the time, savoring every moment.

We found a special spot on one of the beaches that we called our "nest." It was a basket-style hammock we could both lie inside of, hanging from a beam on the cliff above. Swinging in the hammock was peaceful and relaxing, and someone would bring us drinks any time we wanted them. It was a dream.

The memories we made and the intentional time we took for each other are things we will never forget. They enriched our lives and marriage forever. Time away does not need to be extravagant. Even the simplest of adventures can have an incredible impact. Making time to get away together is one of the greatest gifts you can give your marriage.

Heavenly Father, I thank You for my wife. *Being able to get away without distractions fills us both in the best ways. Encourage my wife this week through our time together and our interactions with each other. Help me show her how important she is to me, and may I delight in spending time with her. Show her ways she can make time in her schedule just for us so we can grow closer. Reveal to her any ways that she might be neglecting time in our marriage and strategies she can use to change that. Help me to think of thoughtful and meaningful ways that we can spend time together, and help me to make the time extra special for her. I pray for more moments of peace and calm, and opportunities for us to grow in intimacy. Provide the time, resources, and energy for us to get away. Amen.*

Intentional time away together builds intimacy and trust.

love in action . . .

Together: Be intentional about doing something special together, whether it's a date night or a weekend away.

—— • ——

For her: Plan something special around your wife's interests that you can do with her.

Acknowledgments

To the woman of my dreams, Stefanie. You light up my life. Your passion for restoration over the heart of every person is contagious. I would not have written this book if it weren't for you and your obedience to the call of God. You brought hope to my life and helped restore my relationship with Jesus, and it is the greatest honor of my life to be your husband. I am forever grateful for the dreams I have been able to achieve because of you. I love working with you to help others, and it has brought me alive in purpose, hope, and wholehearted love. Most of all, I am so thankful for being able to walk out my biggest dream of being married to my best friend and the love of my life.

To my children, Shiloh and Asher in heaven. Stefanie and I long to hold you in our arms, but we know you are in safe hands. We love you, and we hope to honor you in how we help and love others. We can't wait to see you in heaven. Say hi to Jesus for us. To any future children God might bless us with: you will be our redemption story. We love you already.

To my parents, John and Kay. Your love for each other, the romance, the fun you continually cultivate show that love can last forever. Thank you for your support and encouragement in making this dream of ours come true. Stefanie and I feel every prayer, and we are so thankful for all the ways that you are there for us in good and difficult times. You motivate us to see the best in each other and to fight for each other and remember that we can all come together in prayer to have peace no matter our circumstance.

To my in-laws, Ed and Susan Stack. I'm forever grateful for the love, sacrifice, example, and generosity you have shown since coming into my life. I am so thankful God chose you to be my in-laws. You have both taught me so much about the servant heart of Jesus in your actions. Your hard work ethic and the way you pour your heart and soul into loving others is such an inspiration. I love you both so much.

To my brothers, Matt and Jesse. Thanks for being great brothers to Stefanie and me! You guys are such a gift. And to Alicia, my sister-in-law, and our niece and nephew, Shirah and Josiah: I am so thankful for each of you, and I appreciate the love and encouragement you always show me. Shirah and Josiah, I'm praying for your future husband and future wife. God has such amazing plans for you!

To my grandma Marcia. Thank you for your constant and consistent love and words of encouragement. You have always been a beacon of light and love. All my memories growing up with you make me think and smile. You are an inspiration for endurance and grace. You have shown me how to overcome and to trust God no matter what season I am in. I am so honored to be your grandson.

To Stefanie's grandma Maryann "Nanny" Miller, to Grandpa "Pappy" Bob Miller (now in heaven), and to our Aunt Cindy. You are the most generous, loving humans. You continually think of others before yourselves. No matter what you have, you look for ways it could bless others. Pappy wrote Stefanie a letter a week for almost ten years, and we received so many at the beginning of our marriage. I know his funny, caring way inspired Stefanie to write and to go after our dreams. Nanny and Cindy, you continually support and love us and make this world a much better place.

To Stefanie's grandpa Bill Stack, and to her grandma Tris Stack and her Aunt Dee (both now in heaven). You continually spoke love and inspiration over us. You cultivated so much fun, joy, and unconditional love.

To Stefanie's sister, Cristina. I'm so grateful for you. To Daniel, my brother-in-law, and our nephews, Daxton and Kadan: we love you so much. You bring so much joy, laughter, and fun into our lives. I'm so proud of you, Daxton and Kadan. God has such amazing plans for your life! We are praying already for your future wives!

To Kara Leonino, Donna Berg, Sarah Atkinson, and the team at Tyndale House Publishers. Thank you for believing in us, for investing in our dreams, and for helping us share our story with the world. Thank you for your intentional feedback and your kindness, and for crying with us, laughing with us, and pushing us to make this book the best it can be.

To Andrea Heinecke, Alex Field, and The Bindery Agency. Working with you has allowed us to dream bigger and make a lifelong dream become a reality. We appreciate you for believing in us and for being our advocates throughout this process.

To my friends, family, and mentors. You are so valued and appreciated. I couldn't have done this project without you. We see you, and we love you so much. Thank you for believing in us.

To our Cultivate Relationship, *Wholehearted Love*, and Love Launchpad women and men, and to all those we have the huge honor of mentoring. Your courage, love, kindness, and growth are so inspiring. We love you and believe in you. We are so proud of you, and we know God is in the midst of redeeming everything in your life!

To our online community. You are loved beyond measure! God has an amazing plan for your life, and we hope this book inspires you to realize that you are not forgotten. The pain and heartbreak you have experienced are not the end of the story. God has so much in store for you! Thank you for your encouragement and support!

About the Author

Caleb Rouse and his wife, Stefanie, are dynamic relationship mentors and digital creators passionately guiding singles and couples toward fulfilling and resilient relationships anchored in faith. With their master's degrees in marriage and family therapy with an emphasis in theology (Stefanie) and in education (Caleb), they offer tailored courses, mentorship, and guidance. These are all rooted in prayer and backed by training in psychology and biblical counseling, encouragement from Christ, and practical strategies for love that lasts. Engaging an audience across multiple social media platforms, Stefanie and Caleb provide daily insights into the transformative power of Jesus' love for all relationship stages. Their vision is a world where we learn to love each other out of God's abundance of love, leading to impactful and joyous relationships.

LET RELATIONSHIP COUNSELORS CALEB AND STEFANIE ROUSE HELP YOU THRIVE IN YOUR RELATIONSHIP WITH YOUR SPOUSE AND WITH GOD!

Stefanie and Caleb Rouse are no strangers to heartache, loneliness, and brokenness. Yet despite personal pain and loss, they've come to discover that God wants us to experience nothing less than wholehearted love—a love that allows us to be fully seen, known, and safe, with Him and with each other. Join them on the journey as they reveal personal stories, practical coaching, and biblical wisdom to guide you toward living—and loving—wholeheartedly.

Learn how to support, love, and care for your husband from a biblical perspective! Stefanie will guide you through compelling stories, prayers, and action steps over the course of a year to enrich your marriage. Refresh your prayer life—and your care for your husband—with these beautiful devotions.

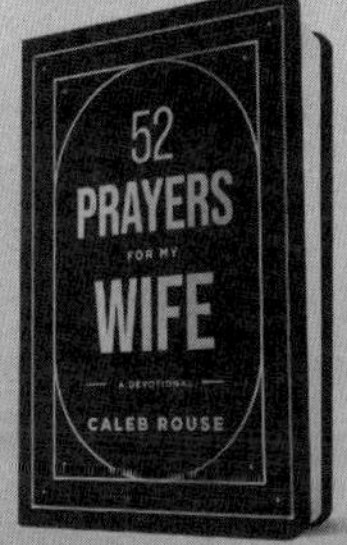

Discover the power of prayer to renew your marriage! Caleb offers prayers, personal stories, and proactive steps to faithfully uplift your wife through each week of the year. Let your words and actions be guided by the Holy Spirit as you love and pray for your wife.

Available wherever books are sold.

CP2004